AF465958

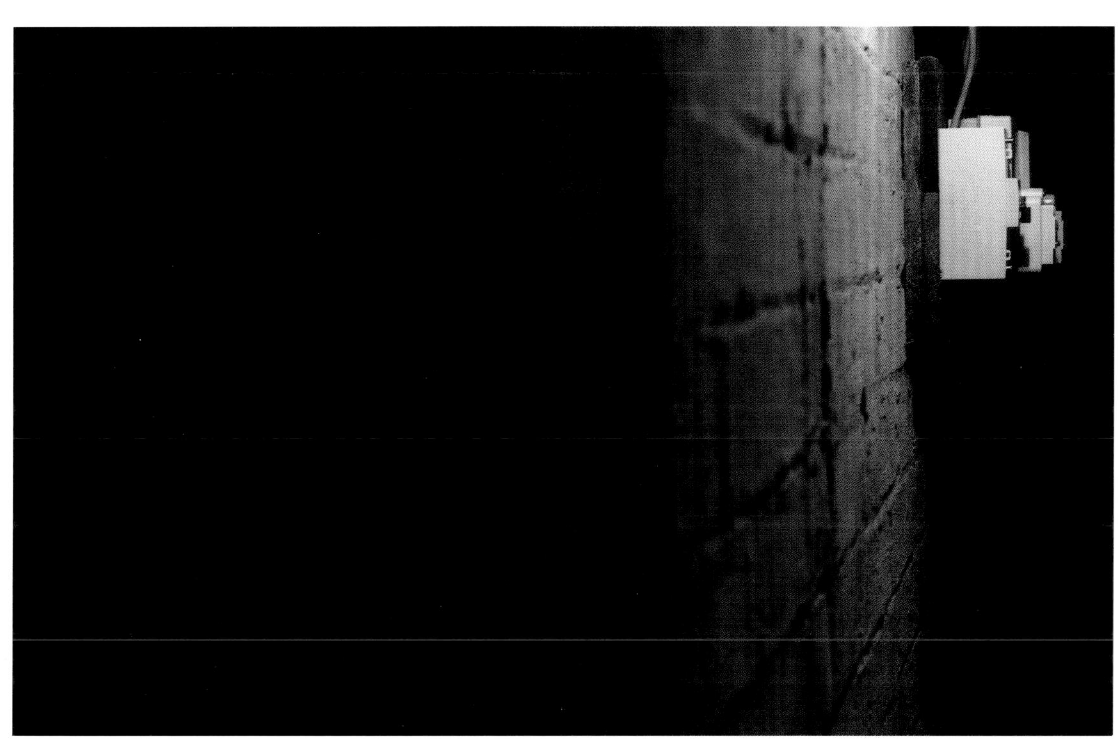

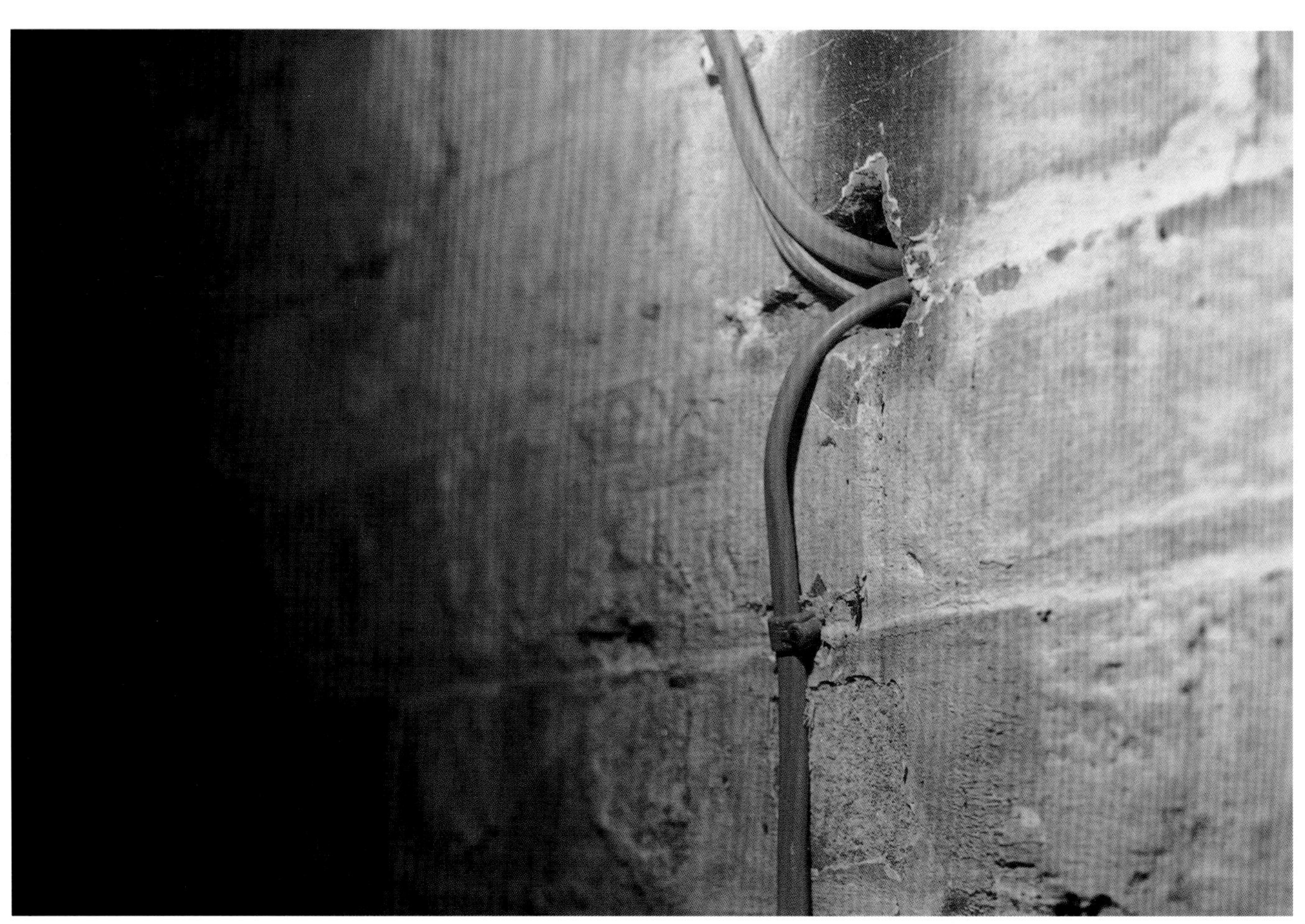

Interior Light

photographs

Lynn Silverman

afterword

Yve Lomax

DEWI LEWIS
PUBLISHING

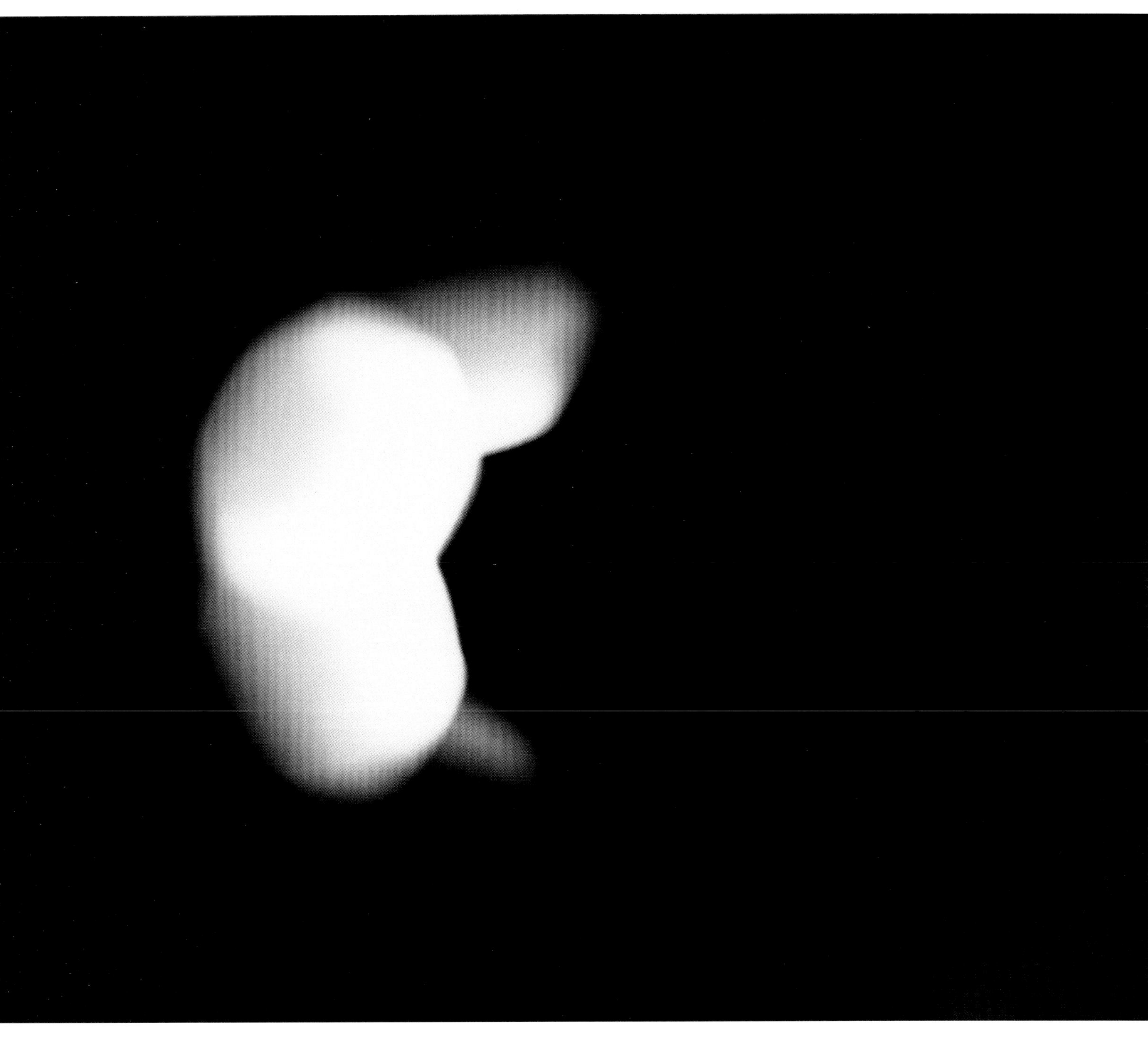

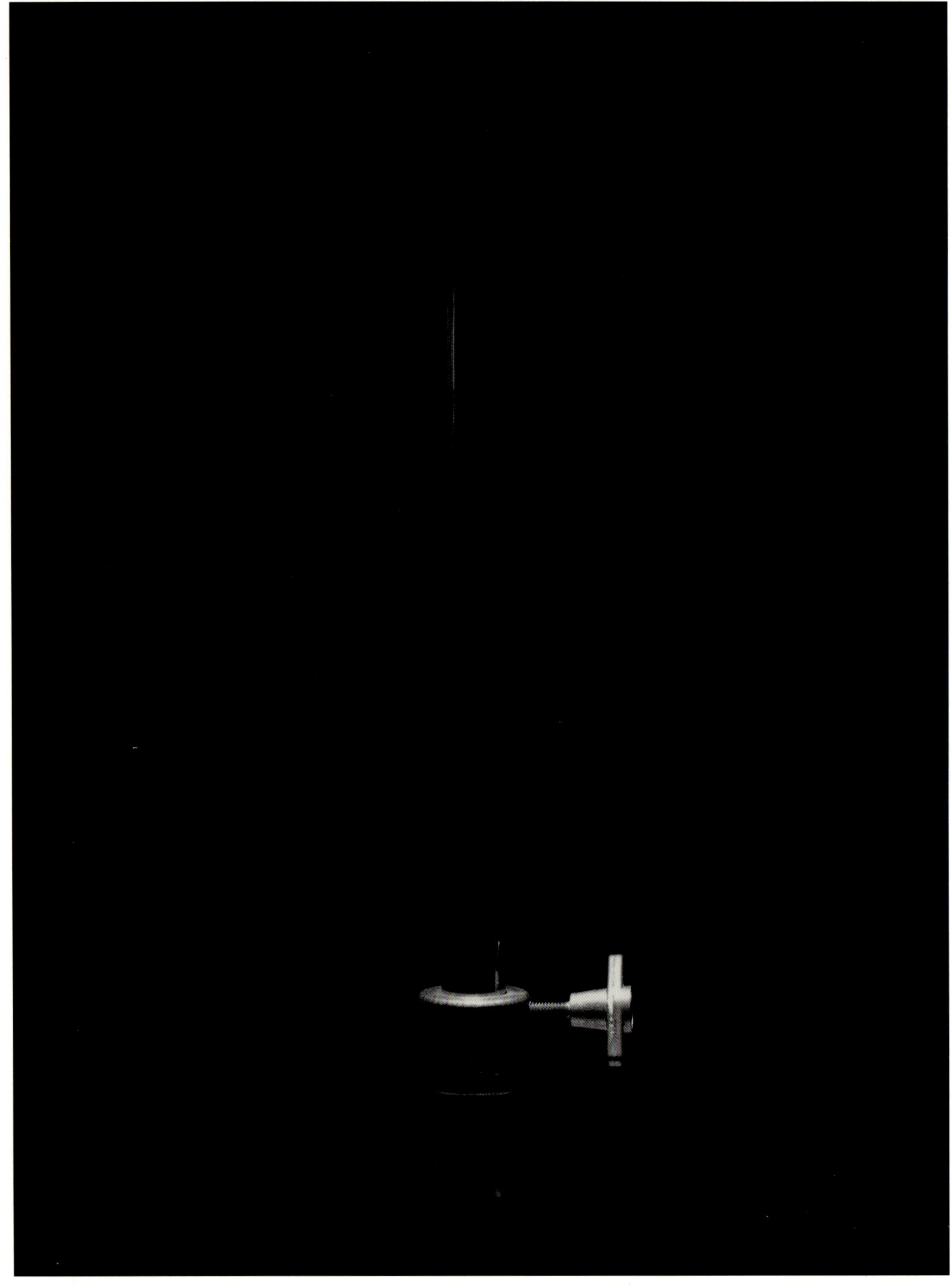

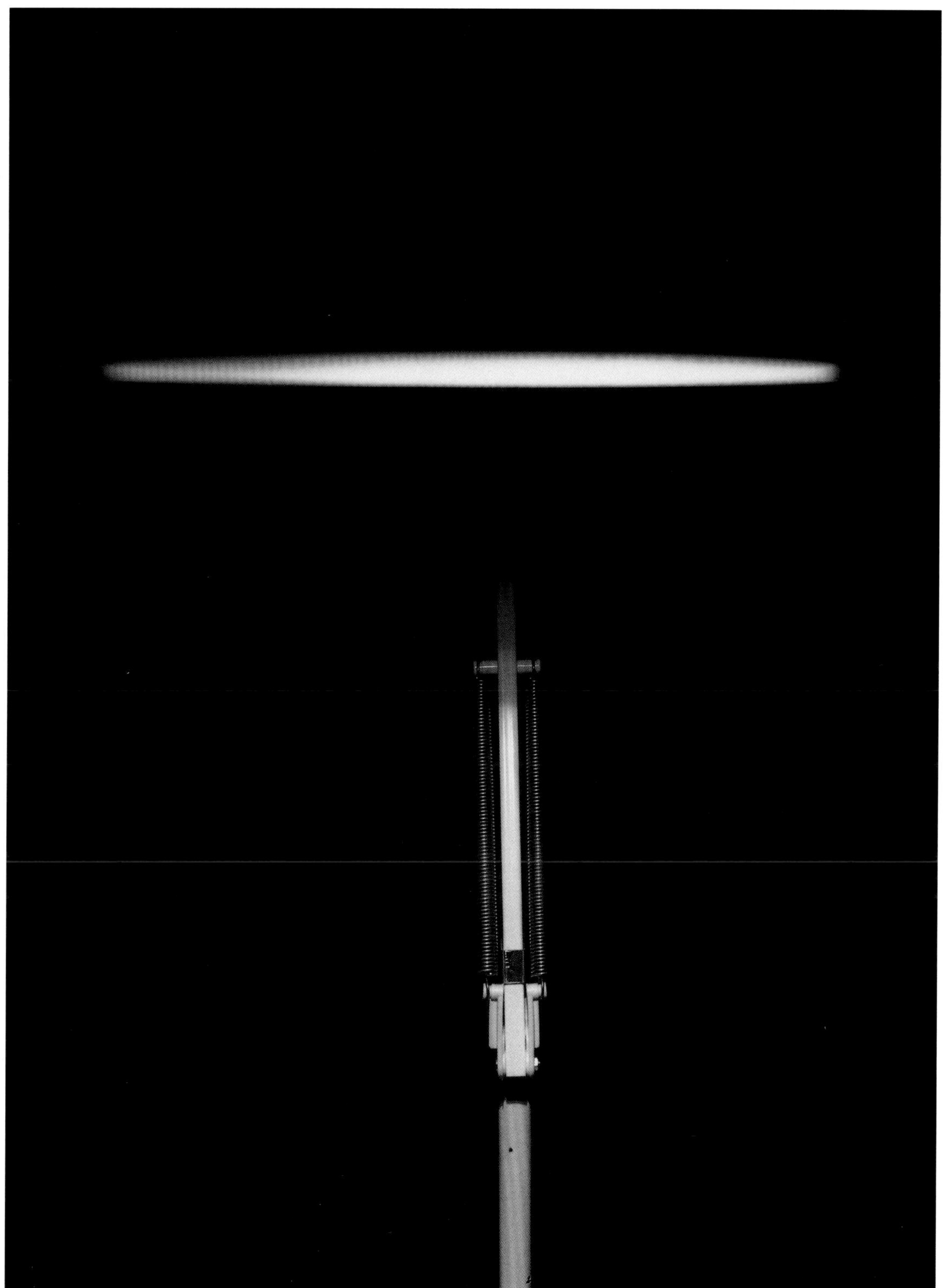

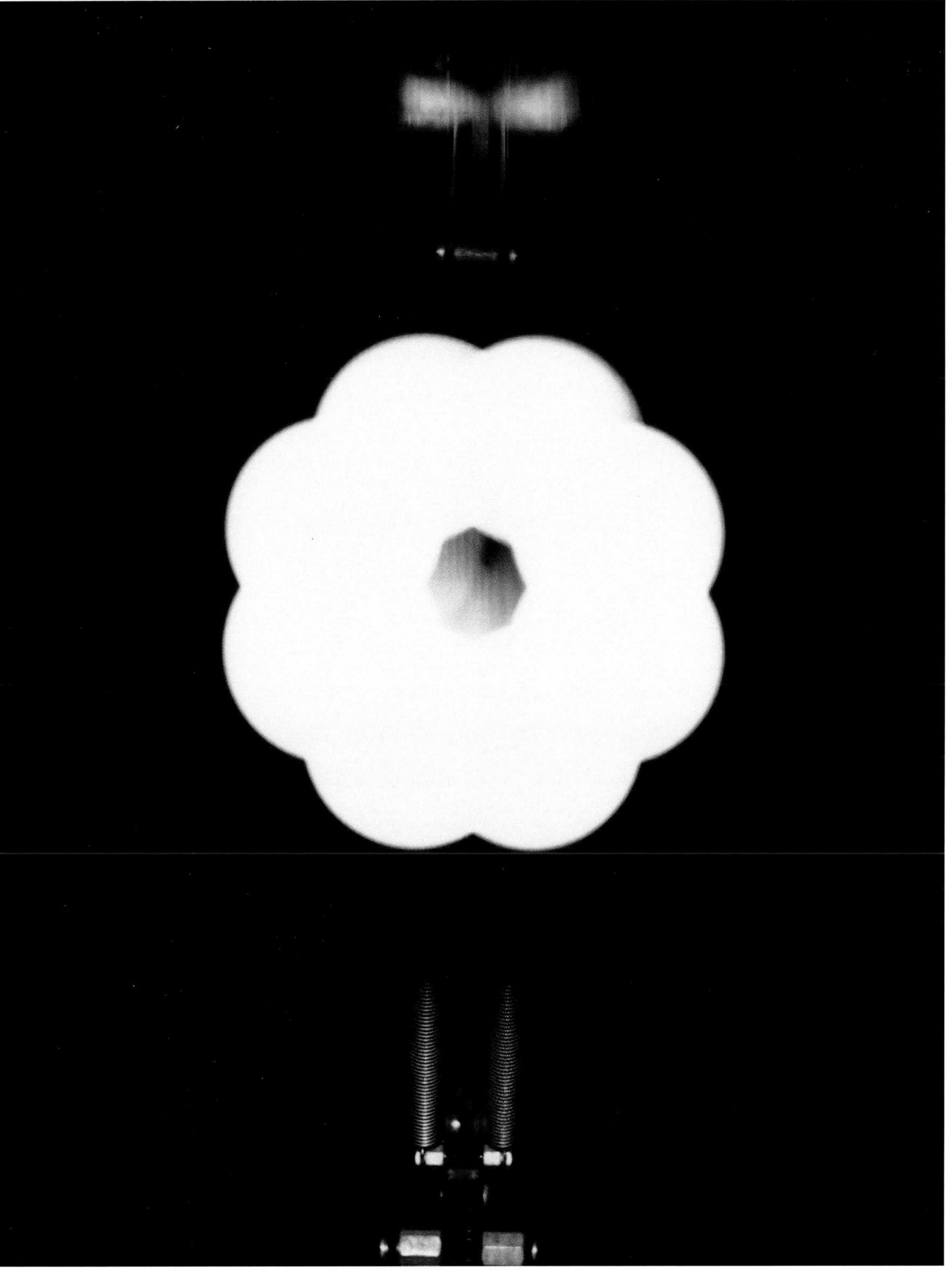

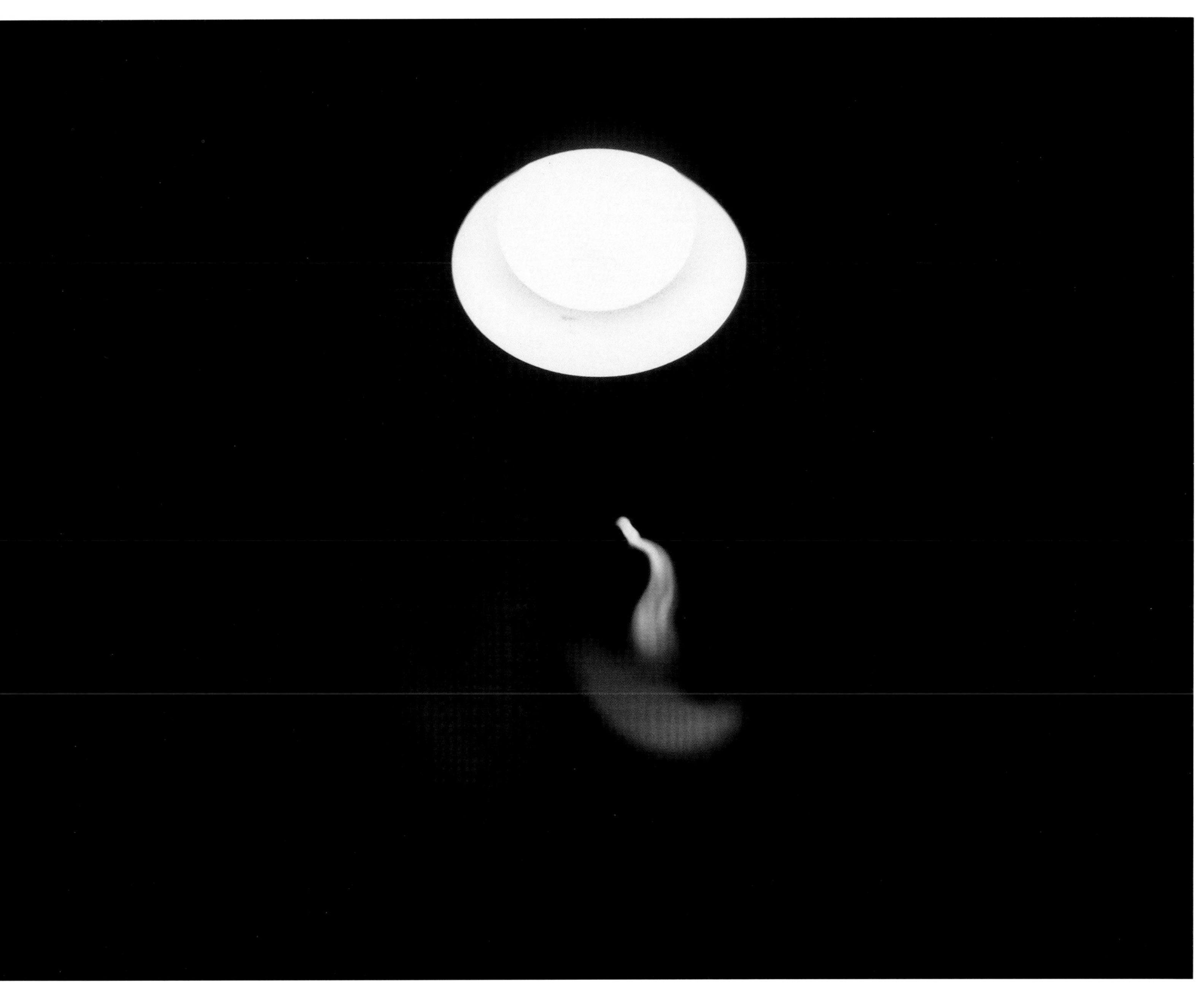

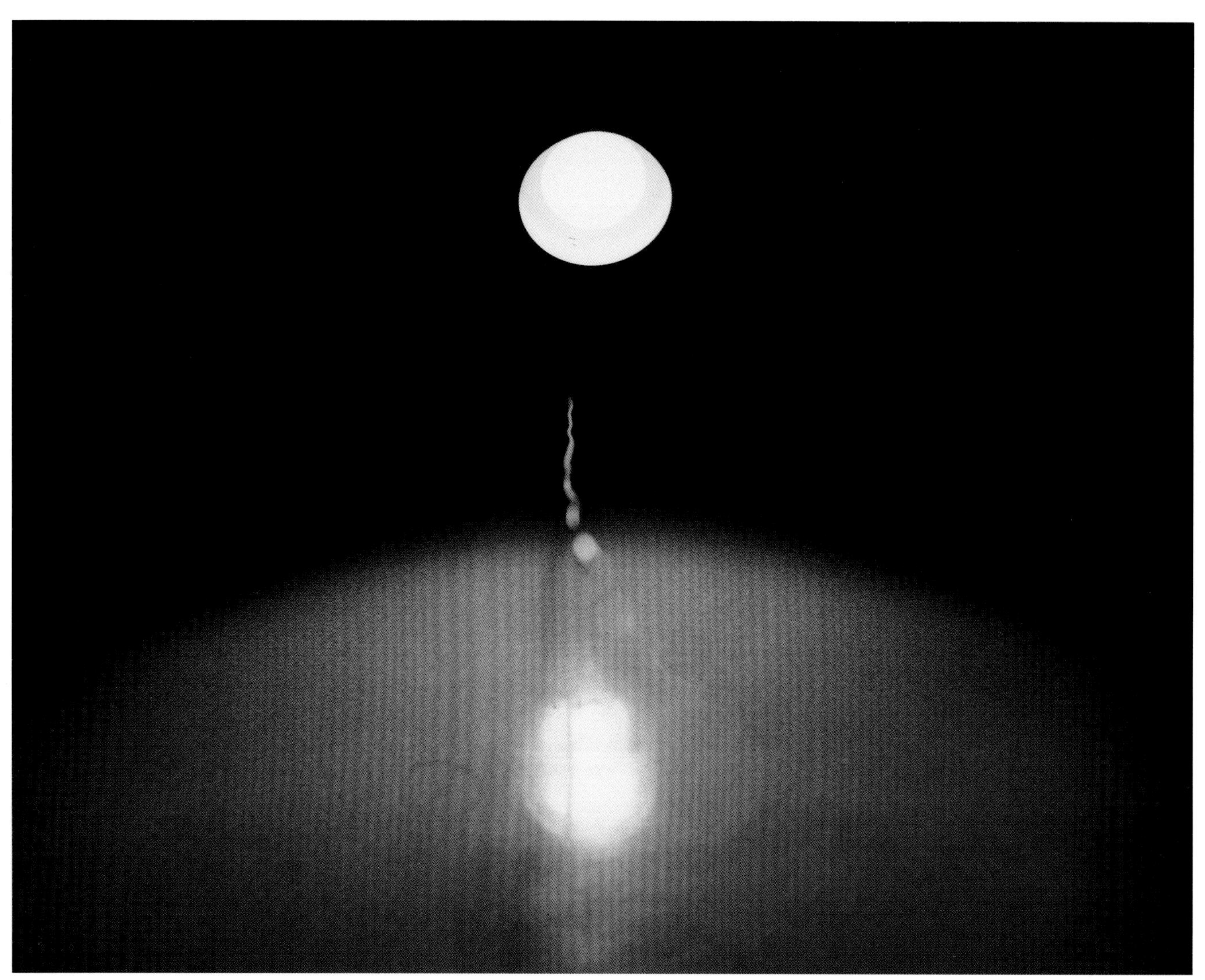

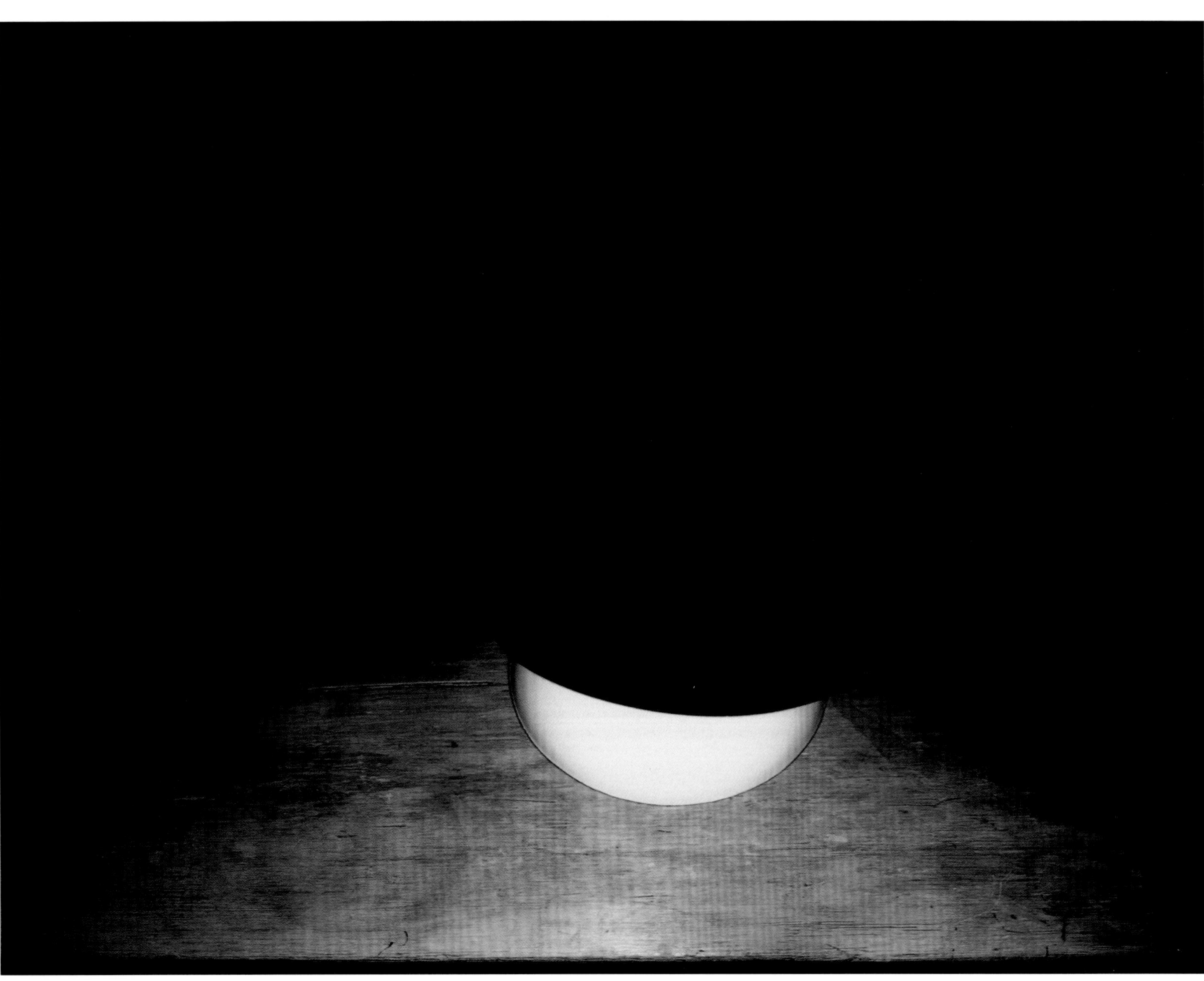

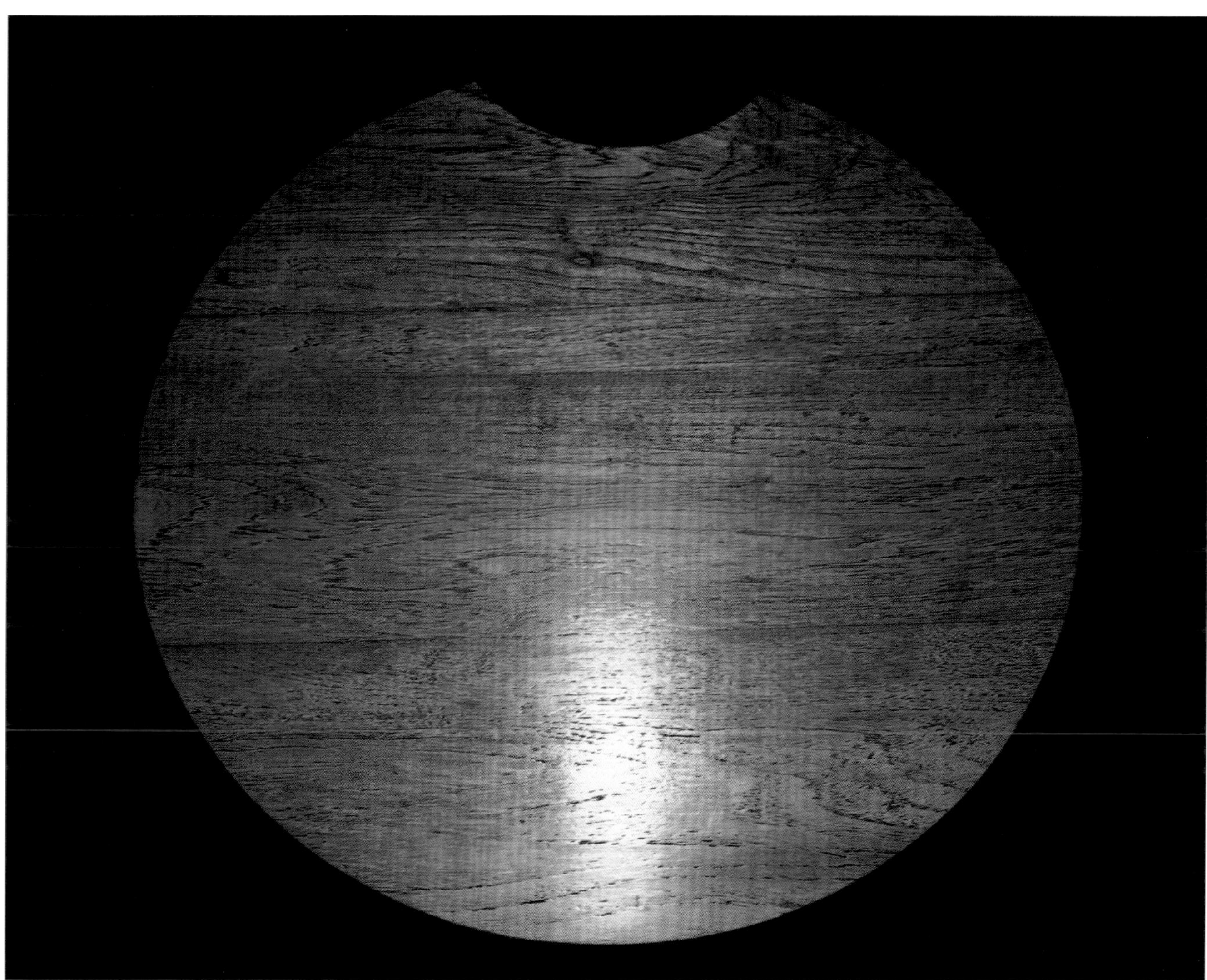

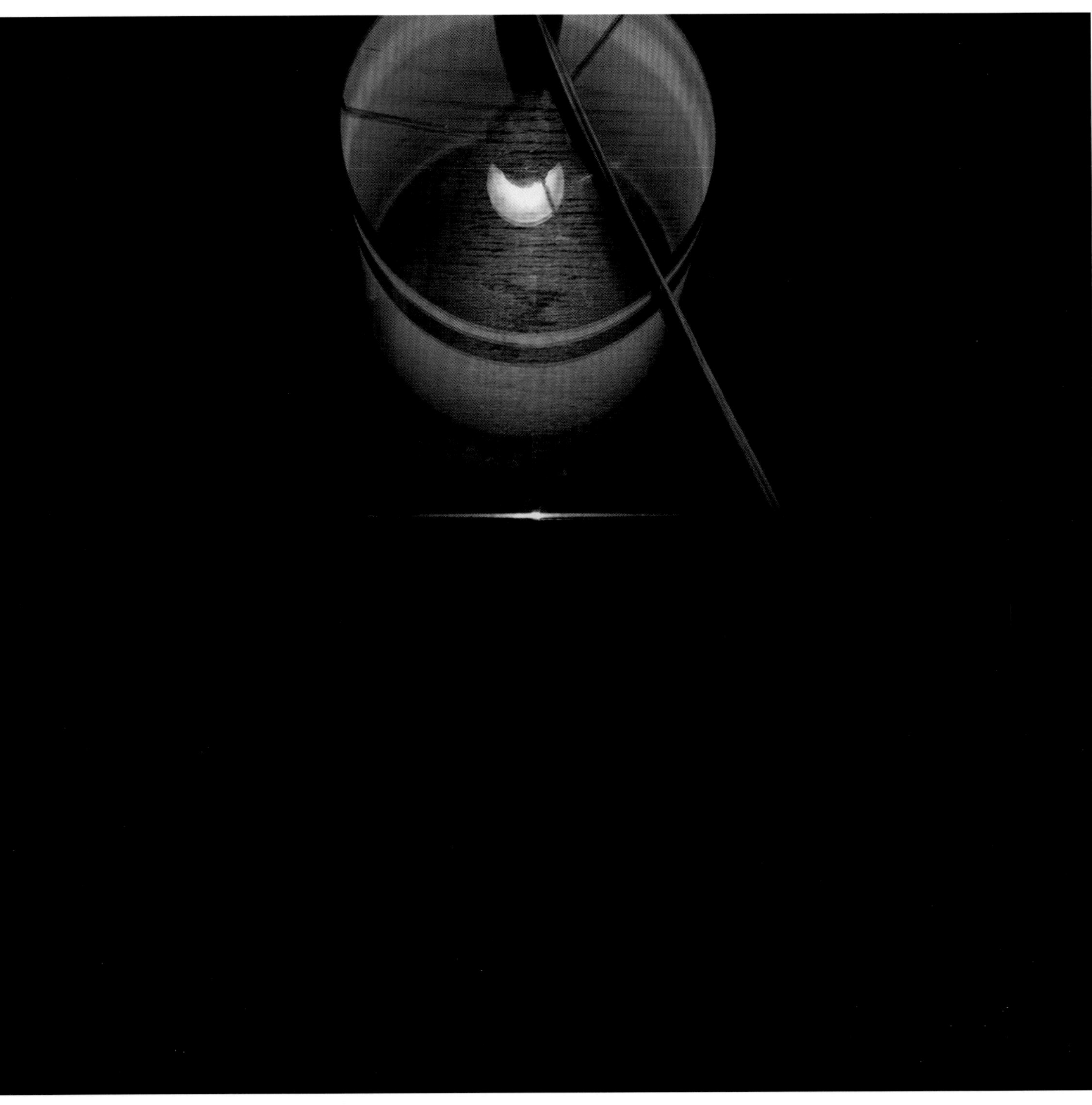

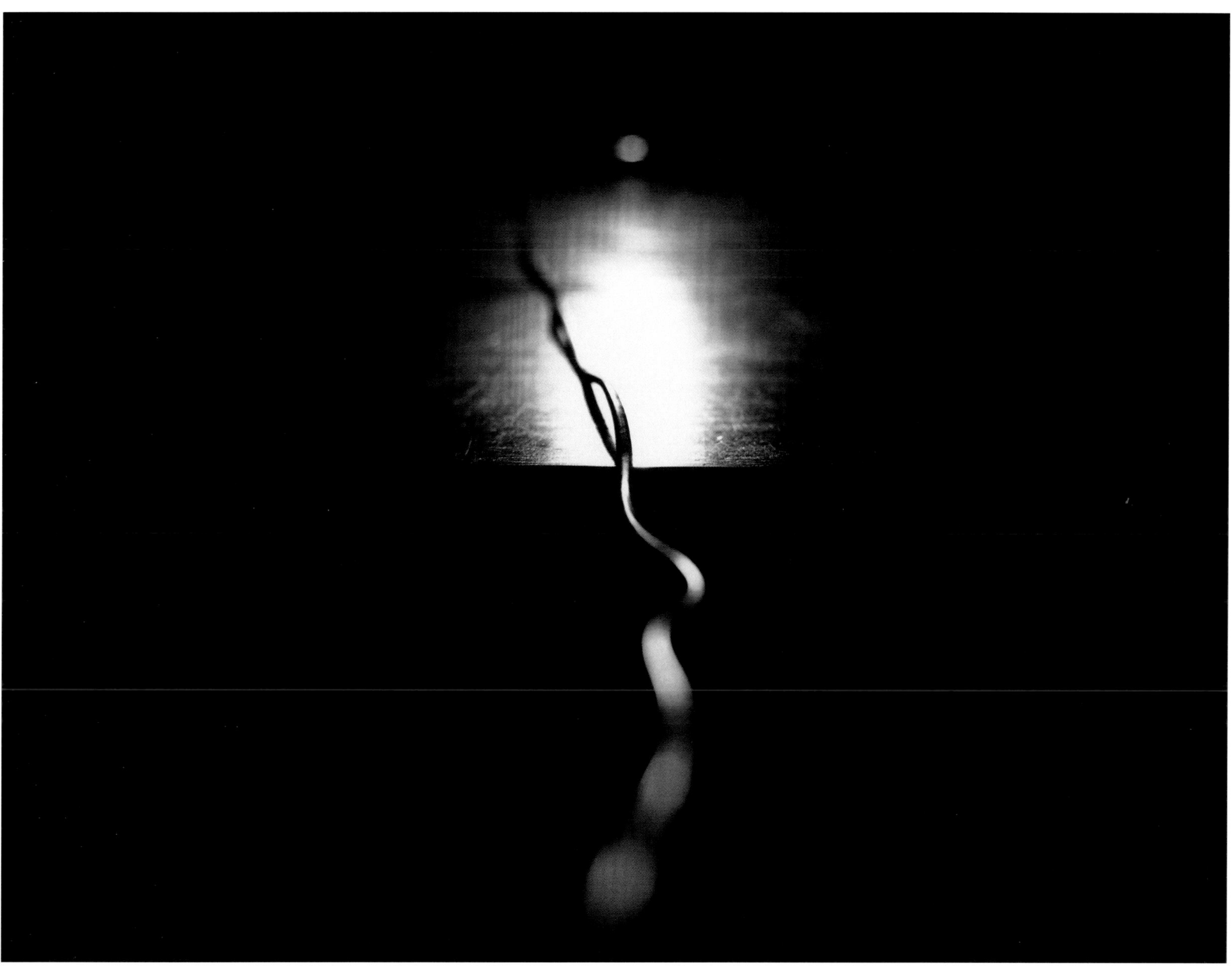

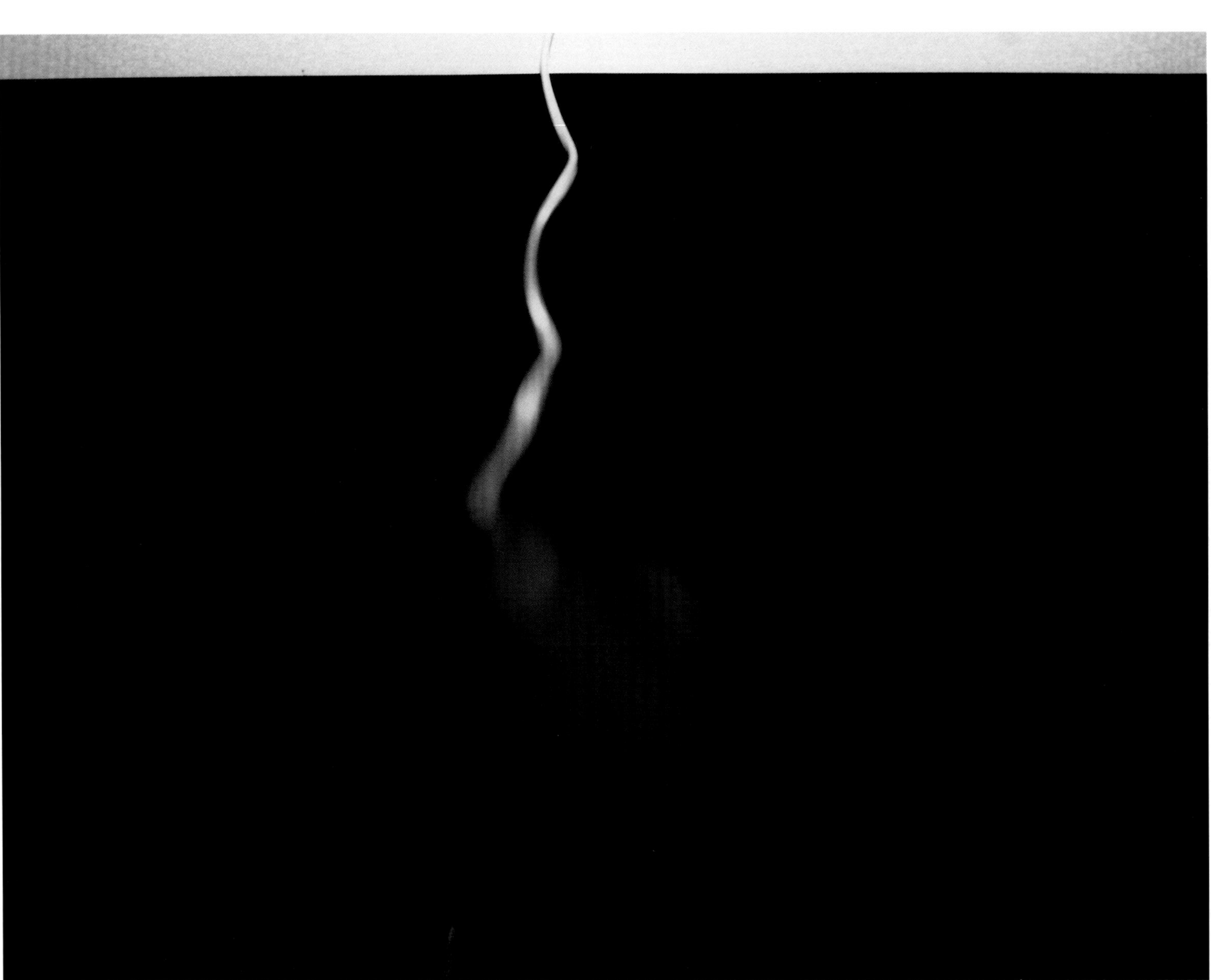

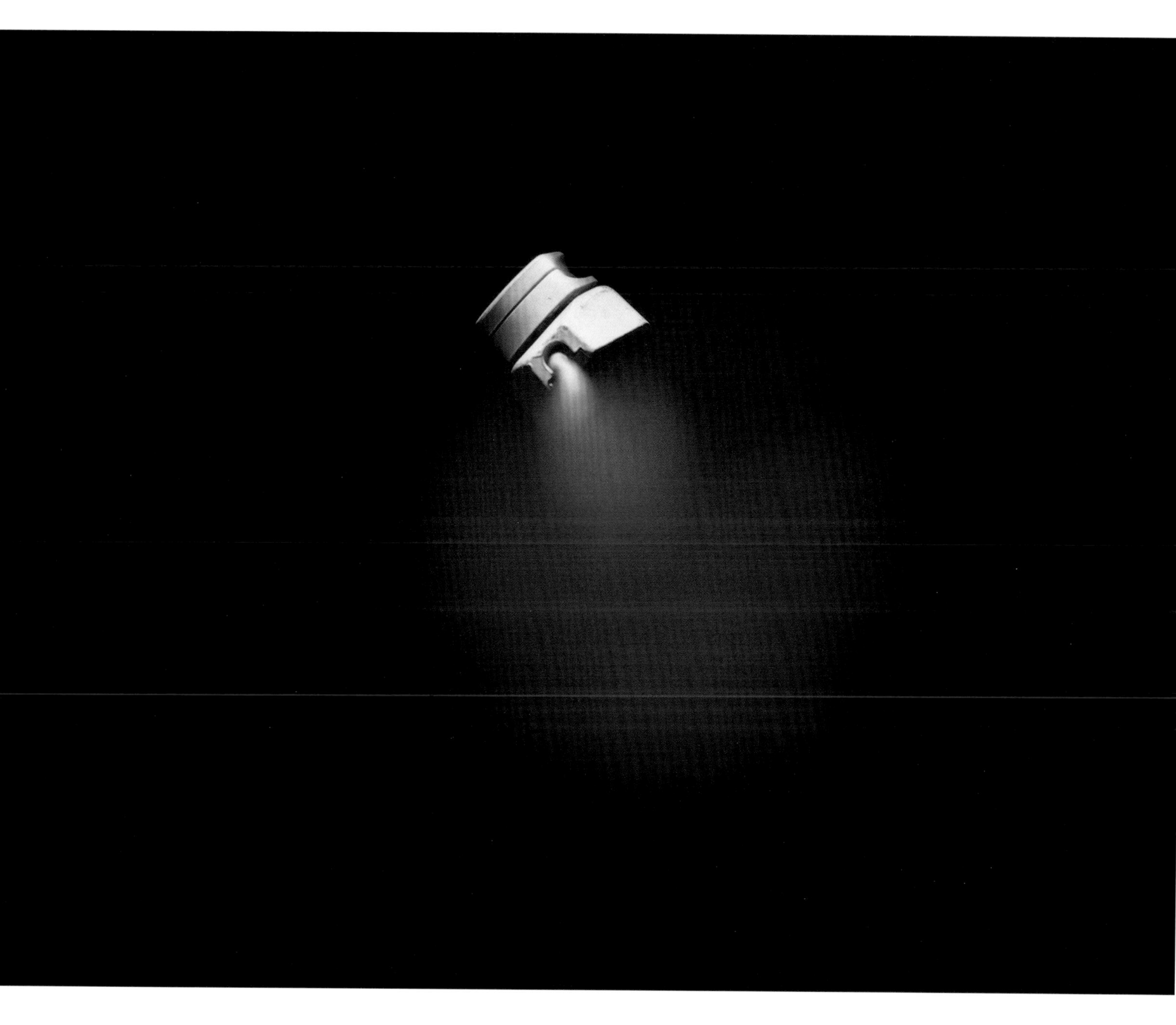

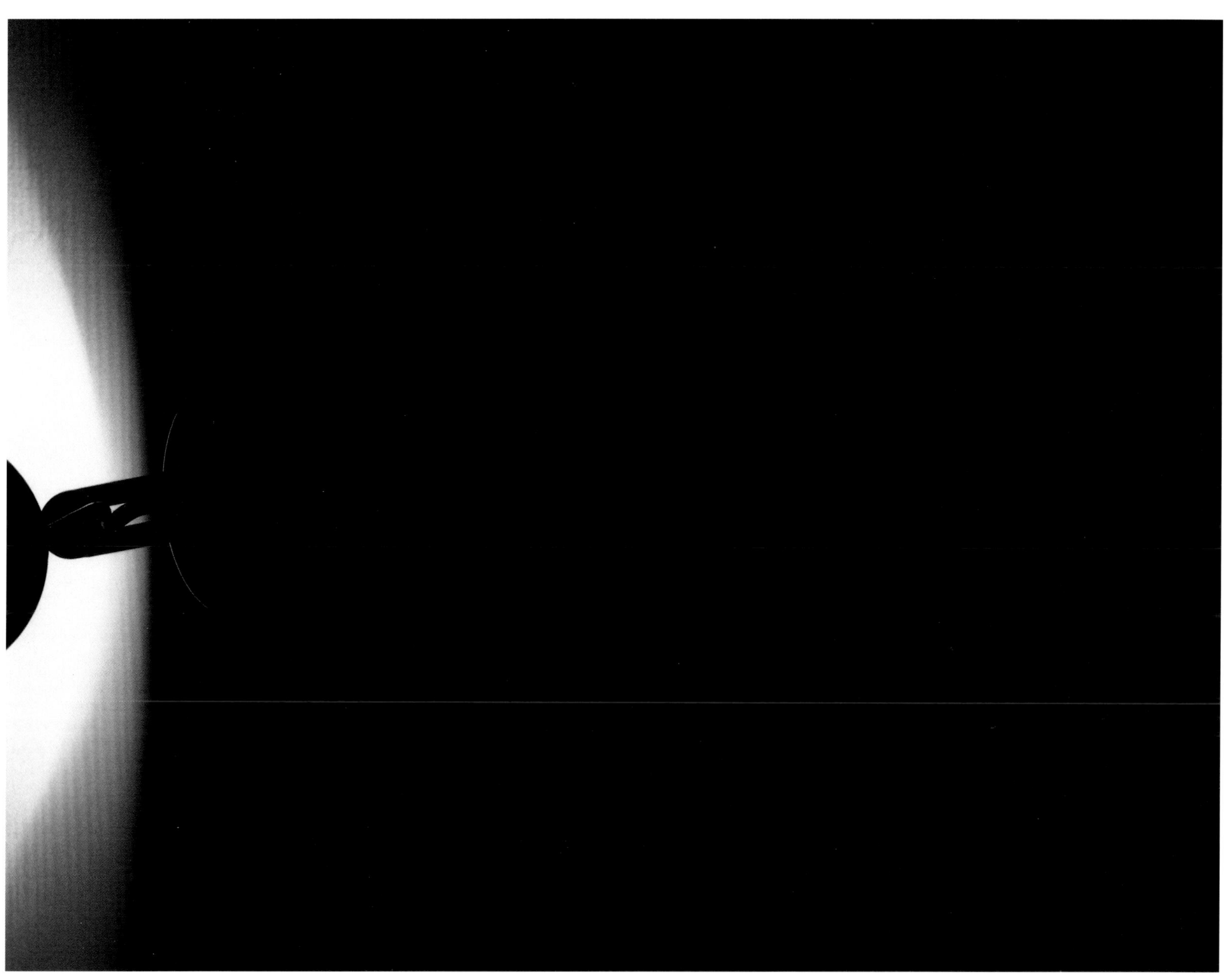

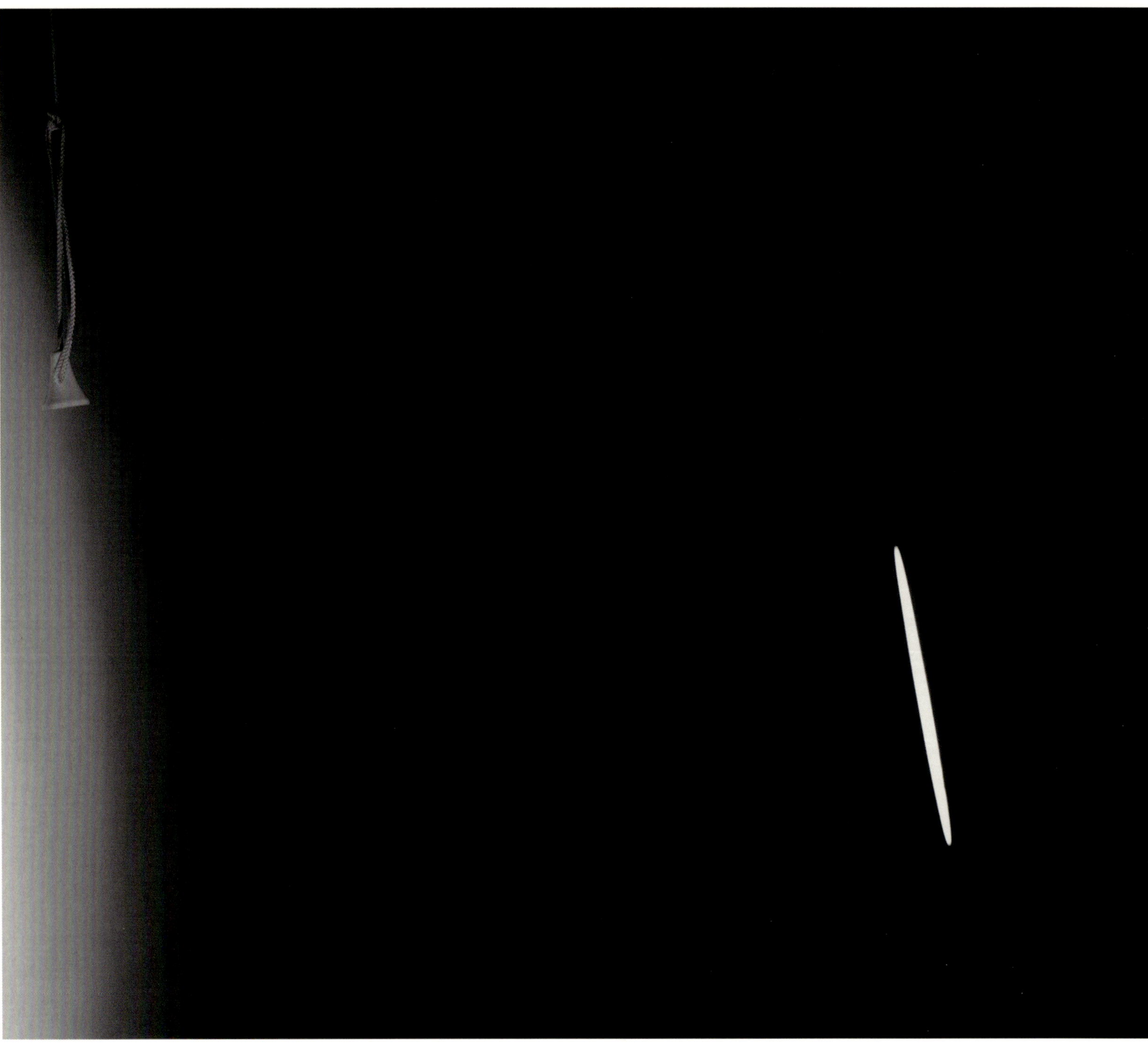

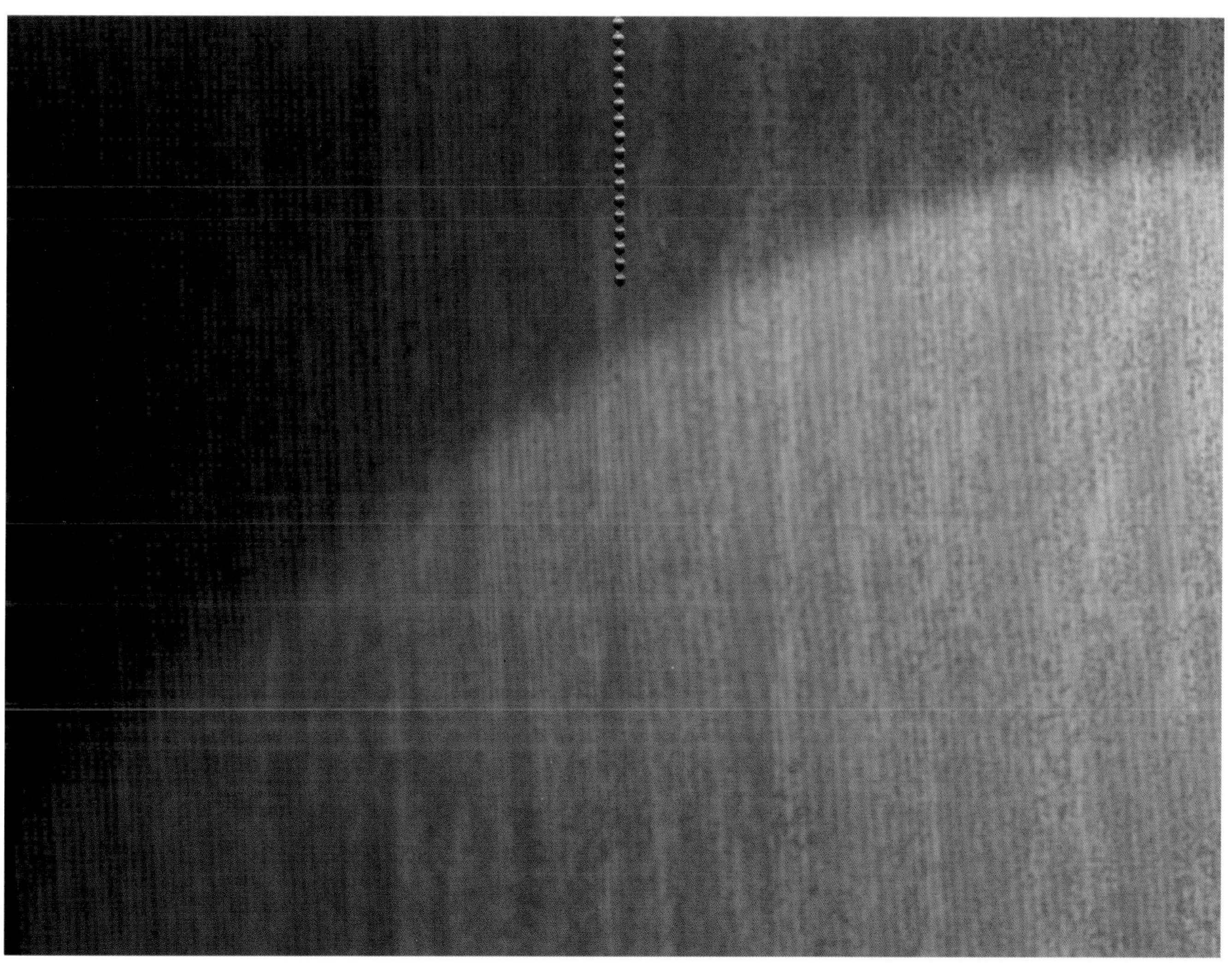

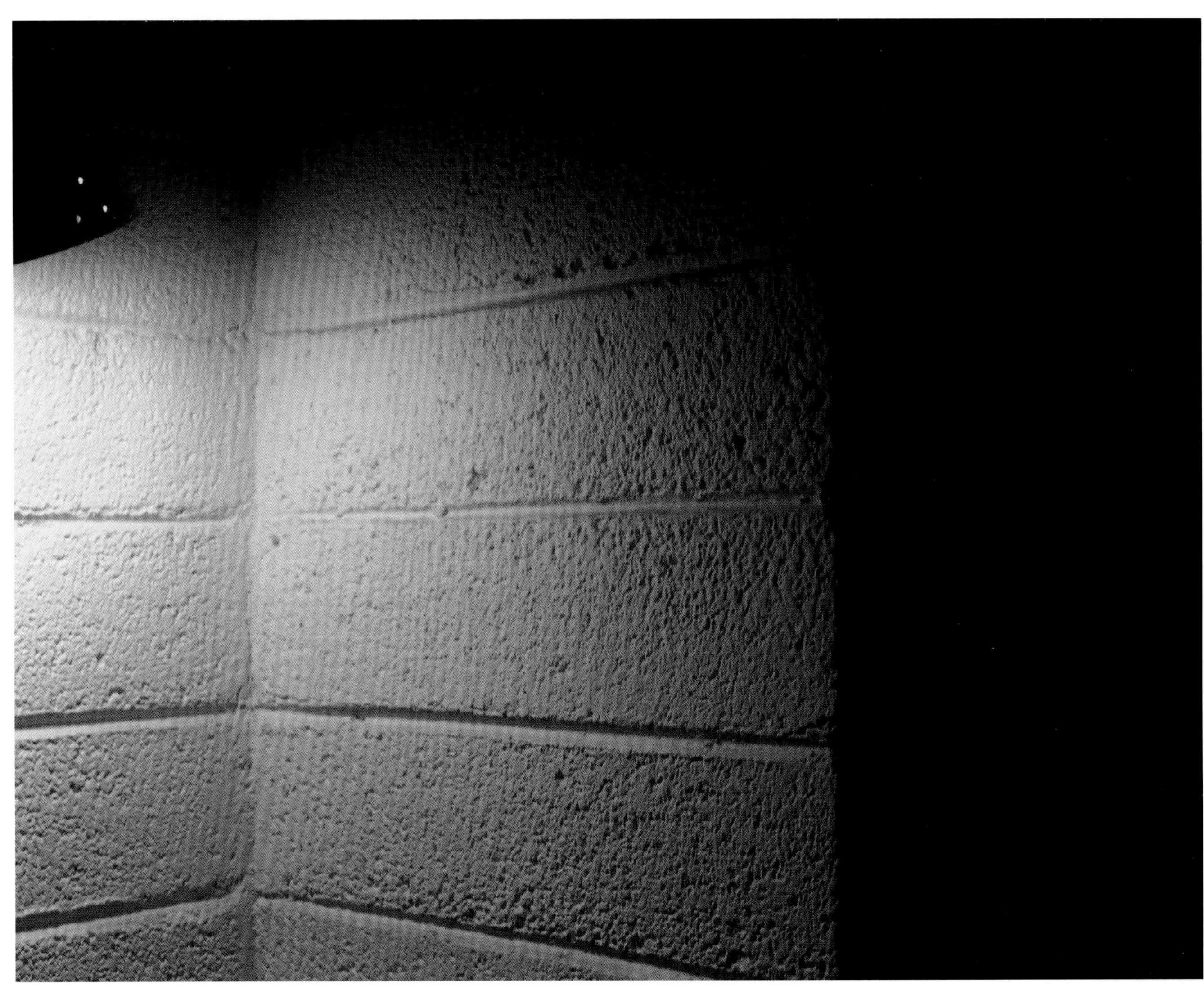

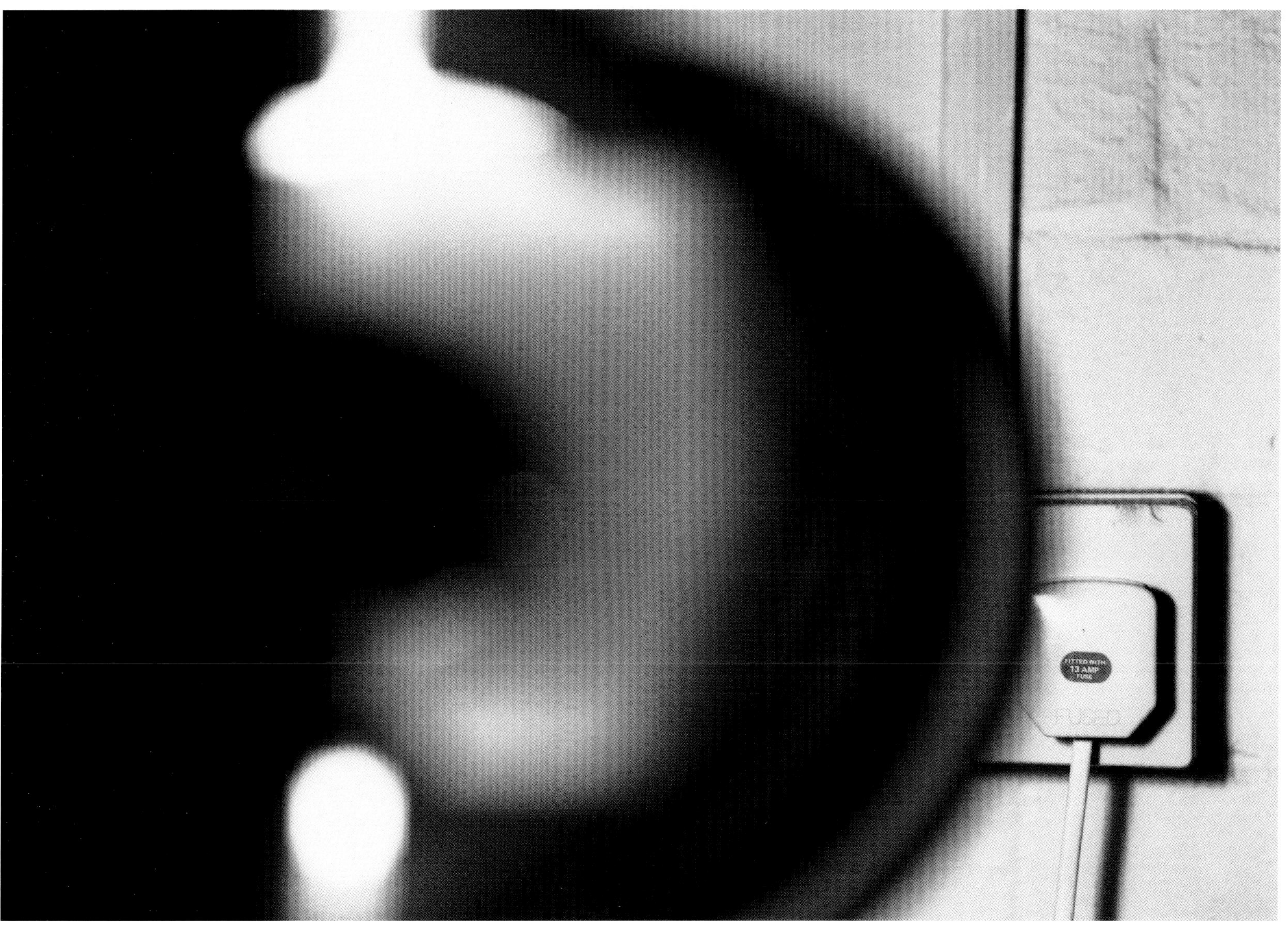
FITTED WITH
13 AMP
FUSED

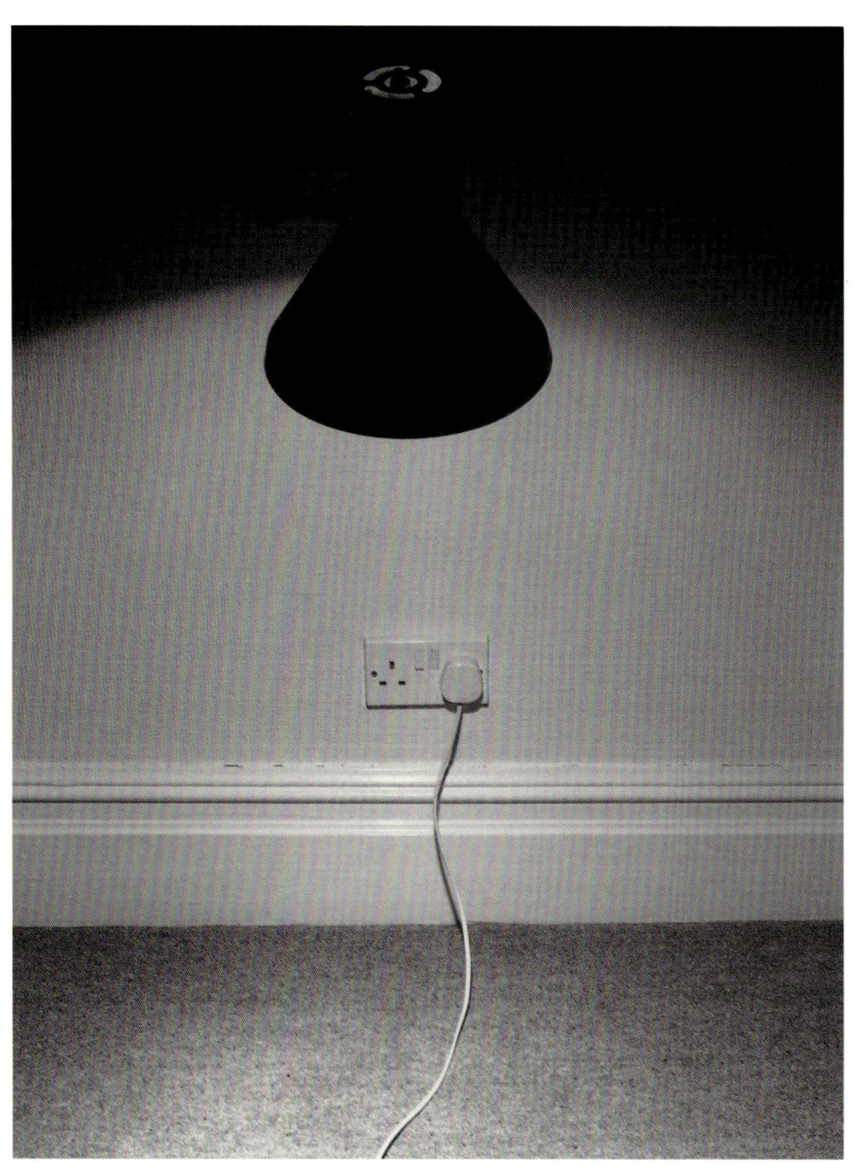

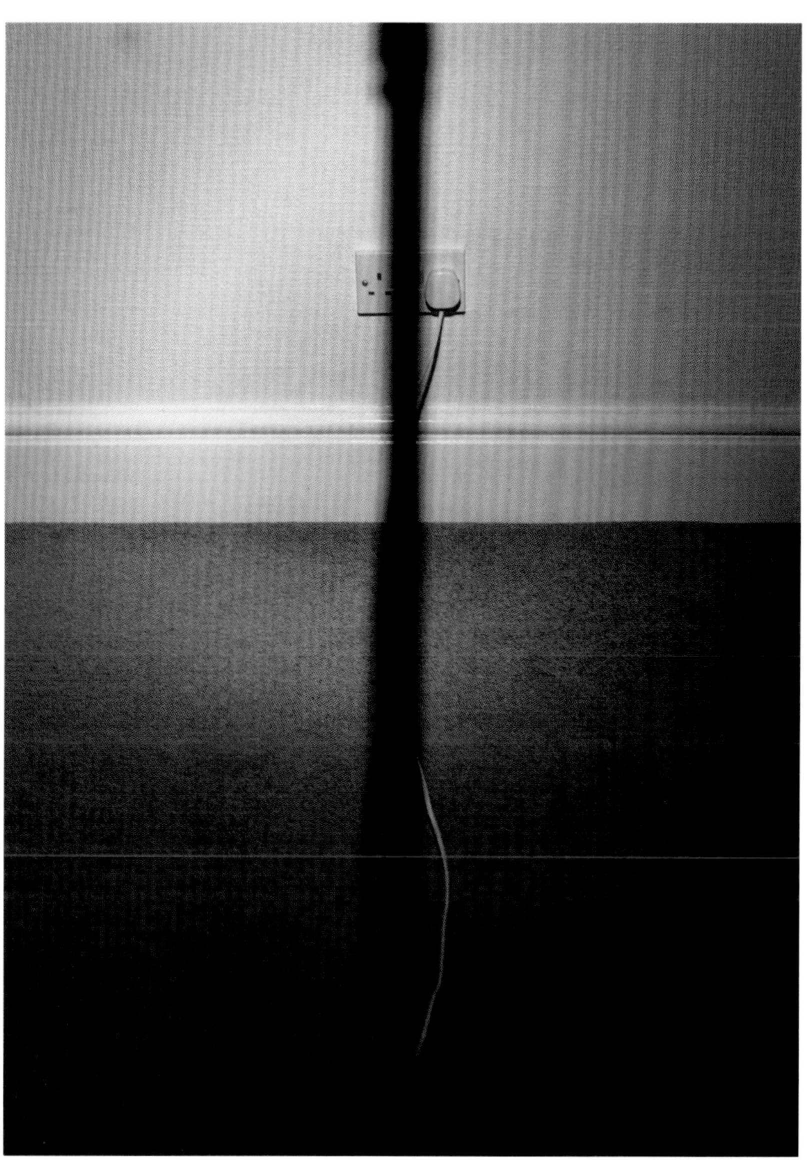

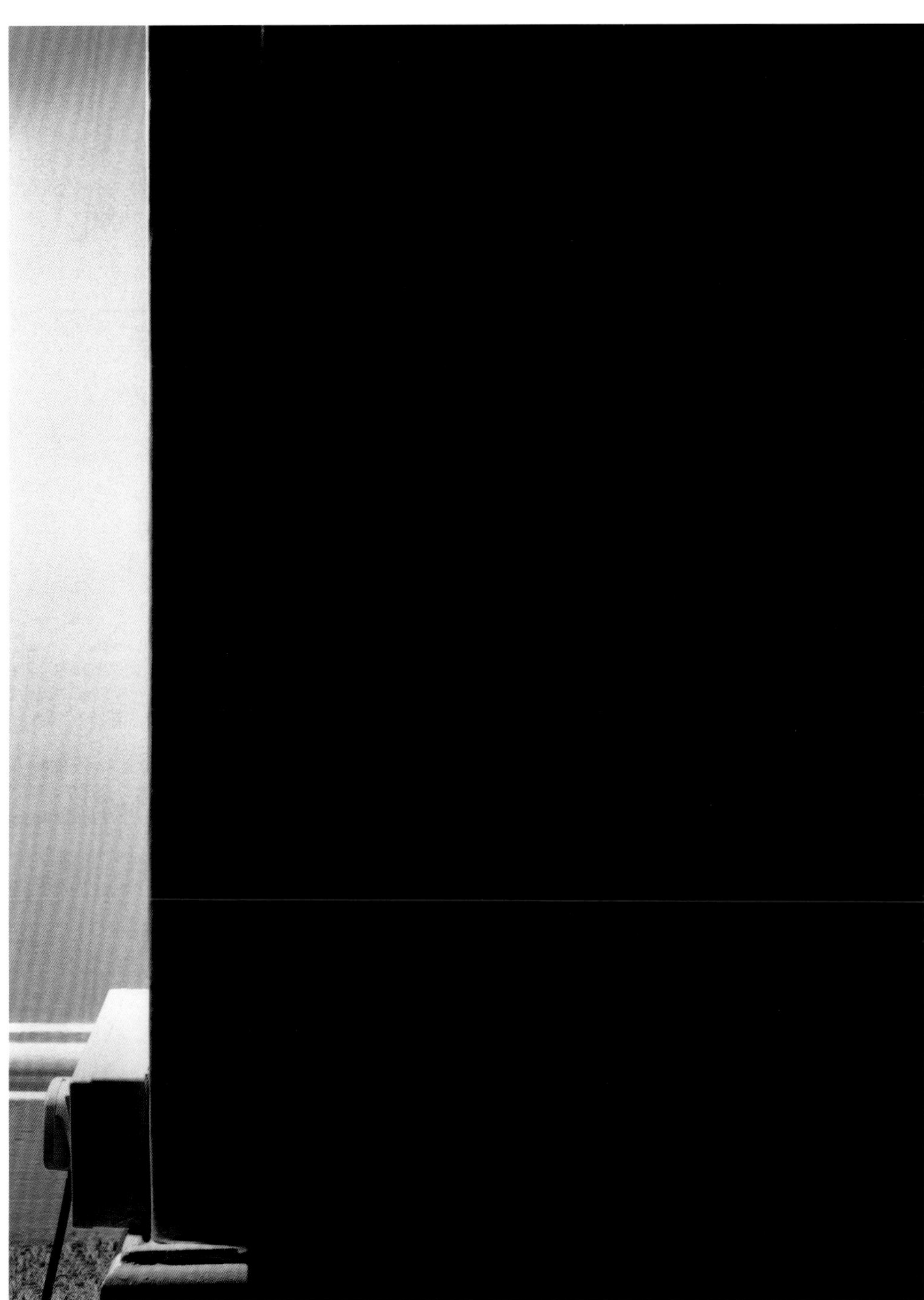

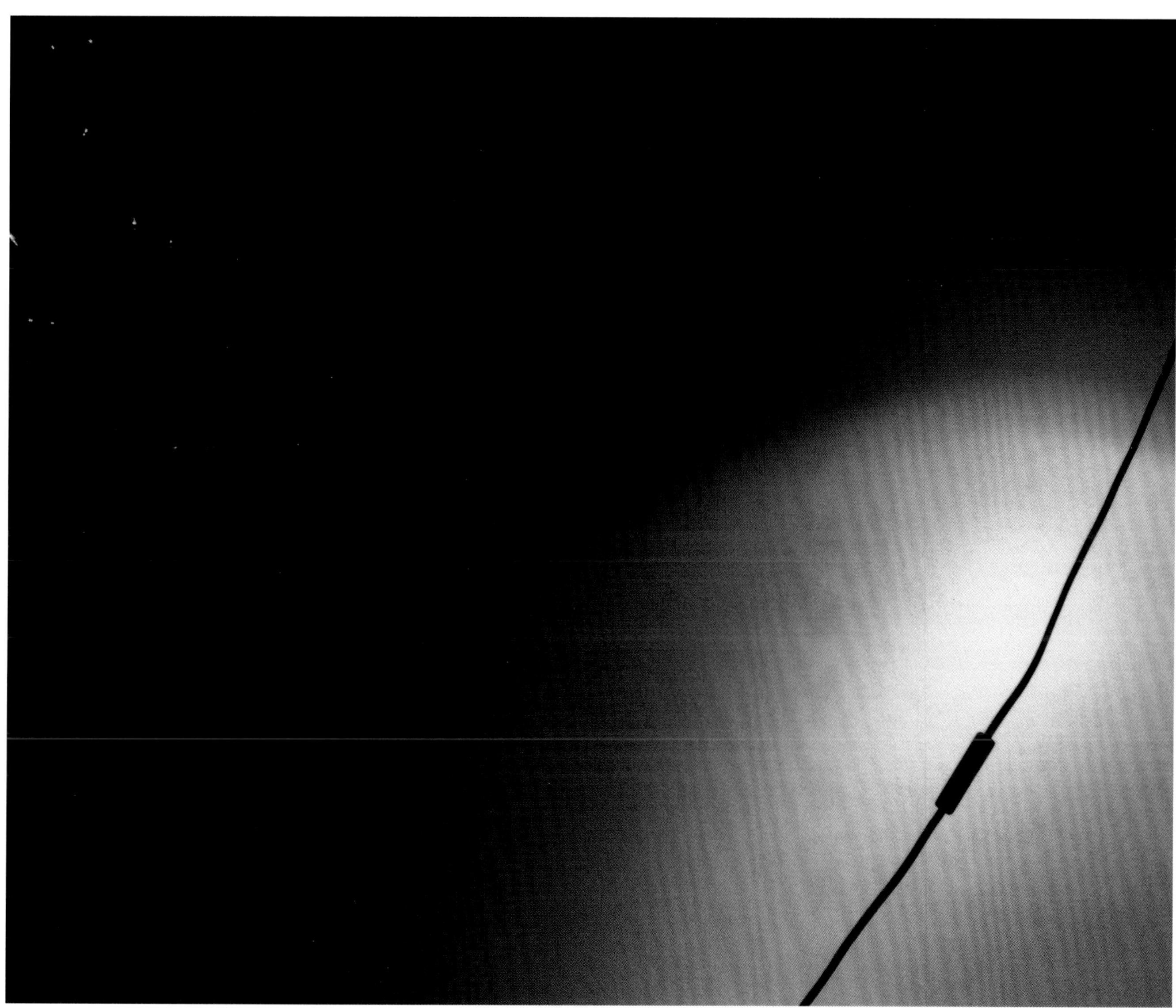

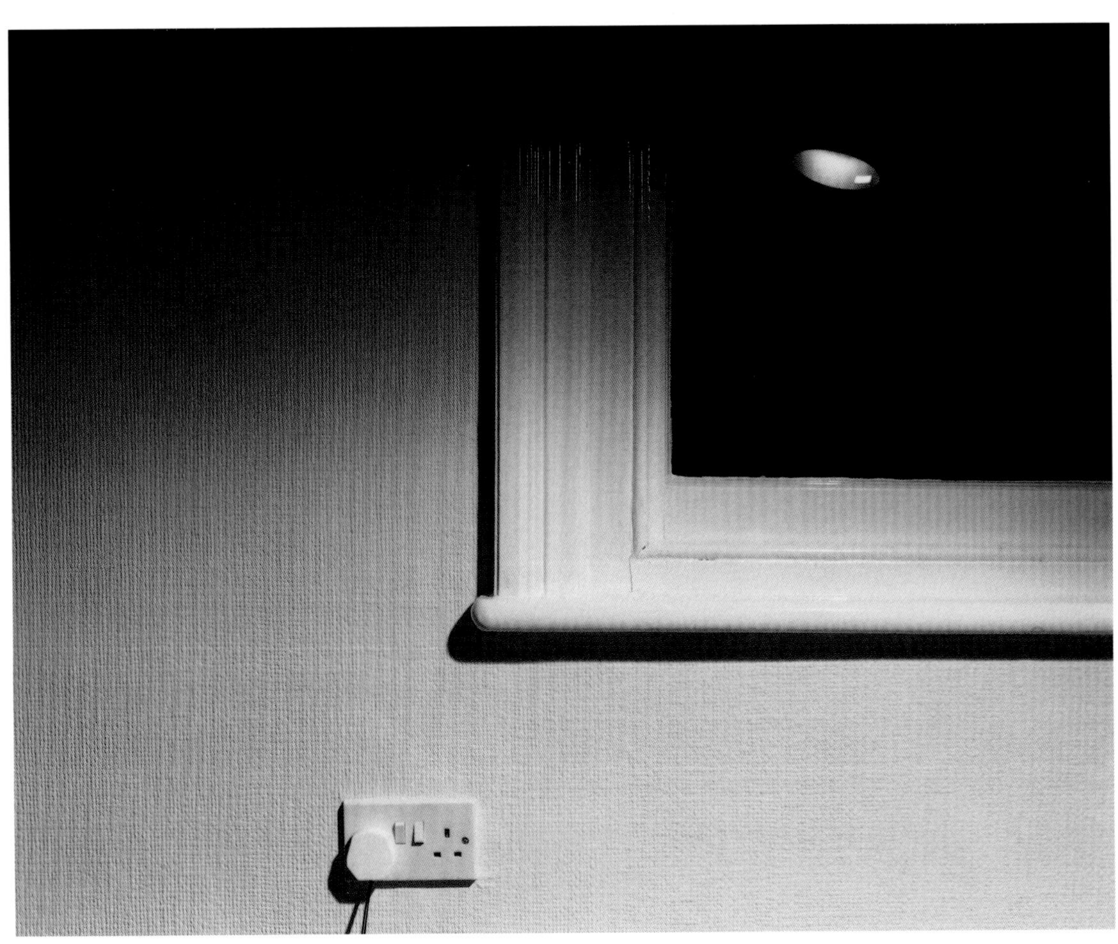

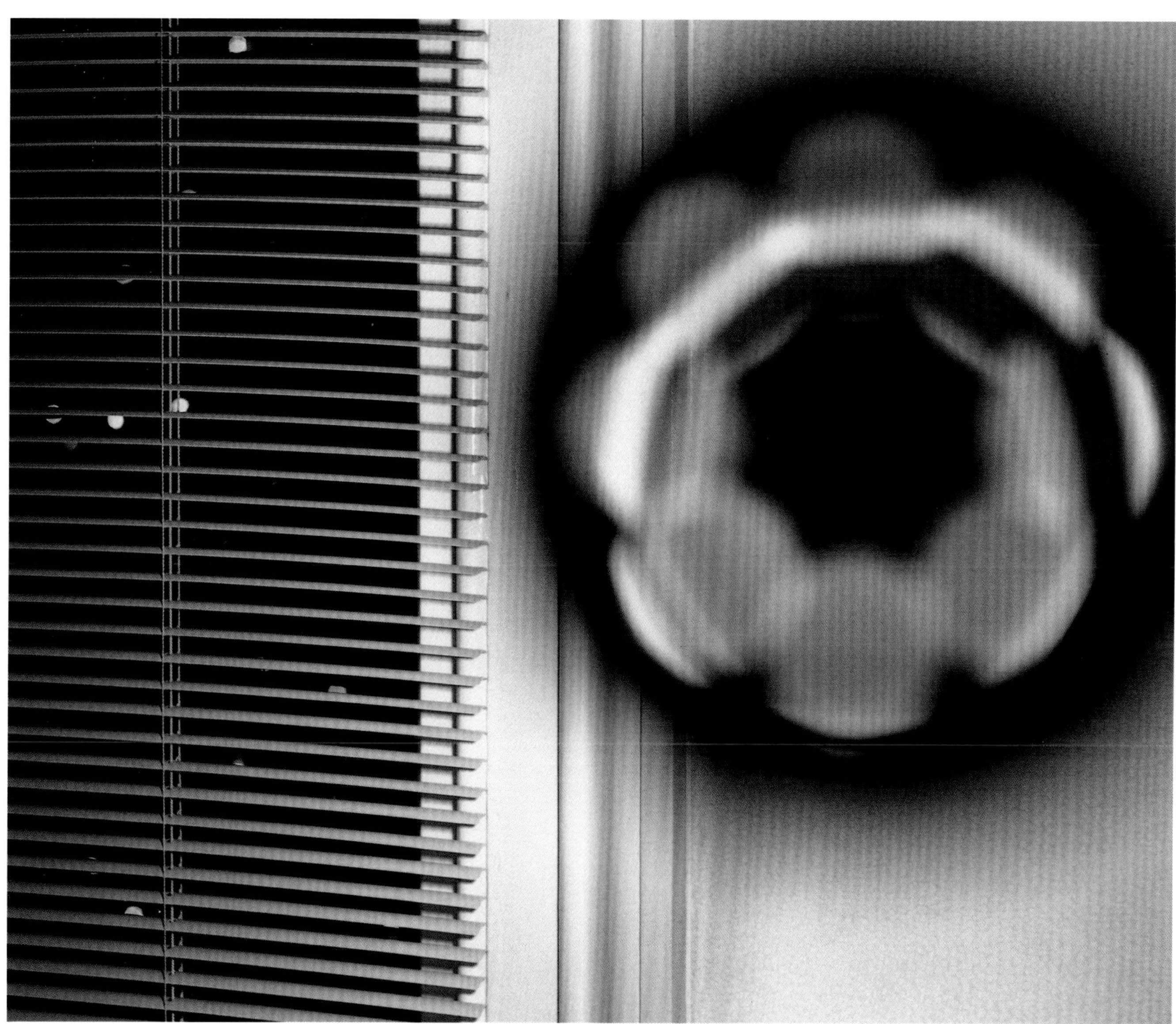

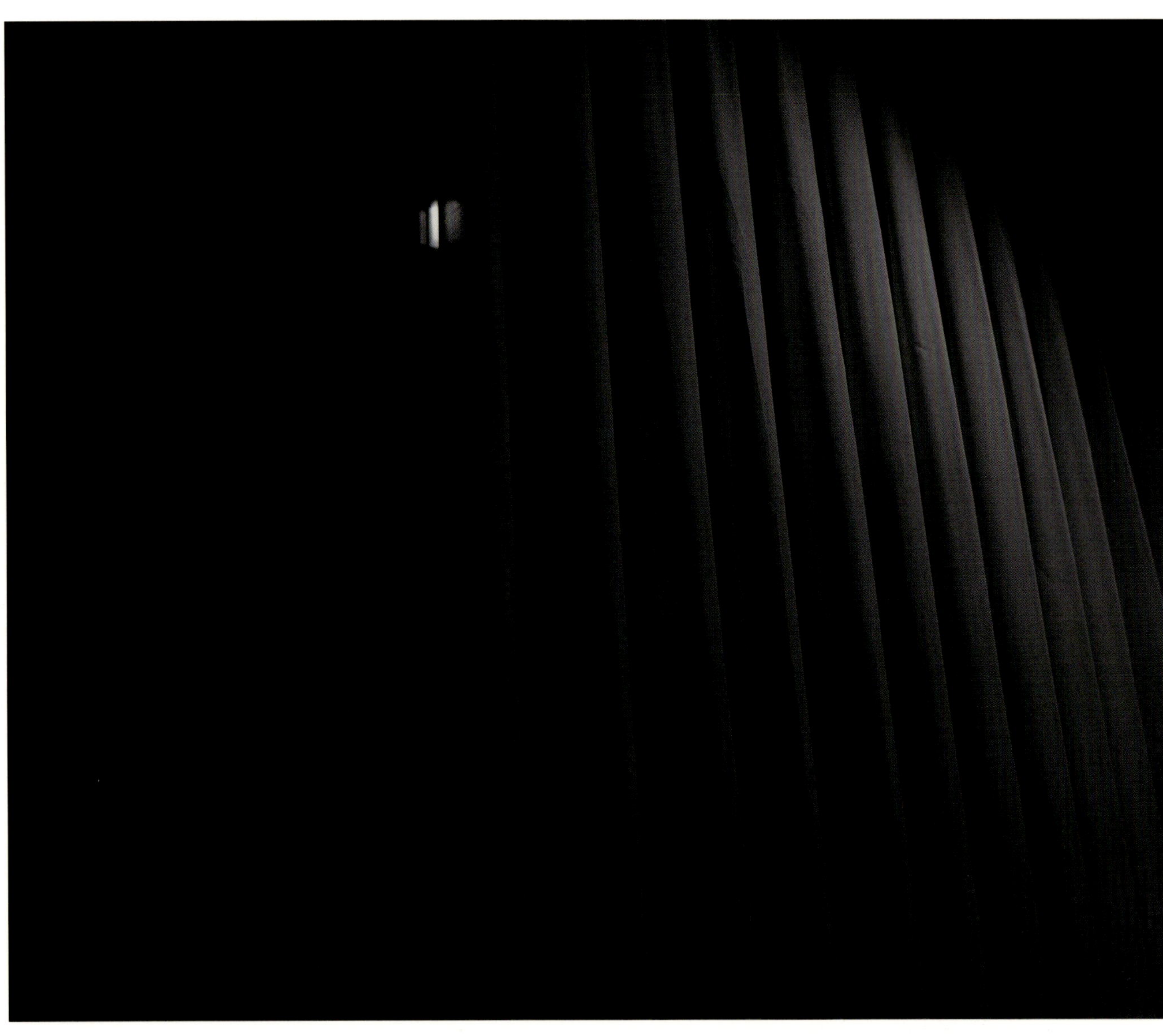

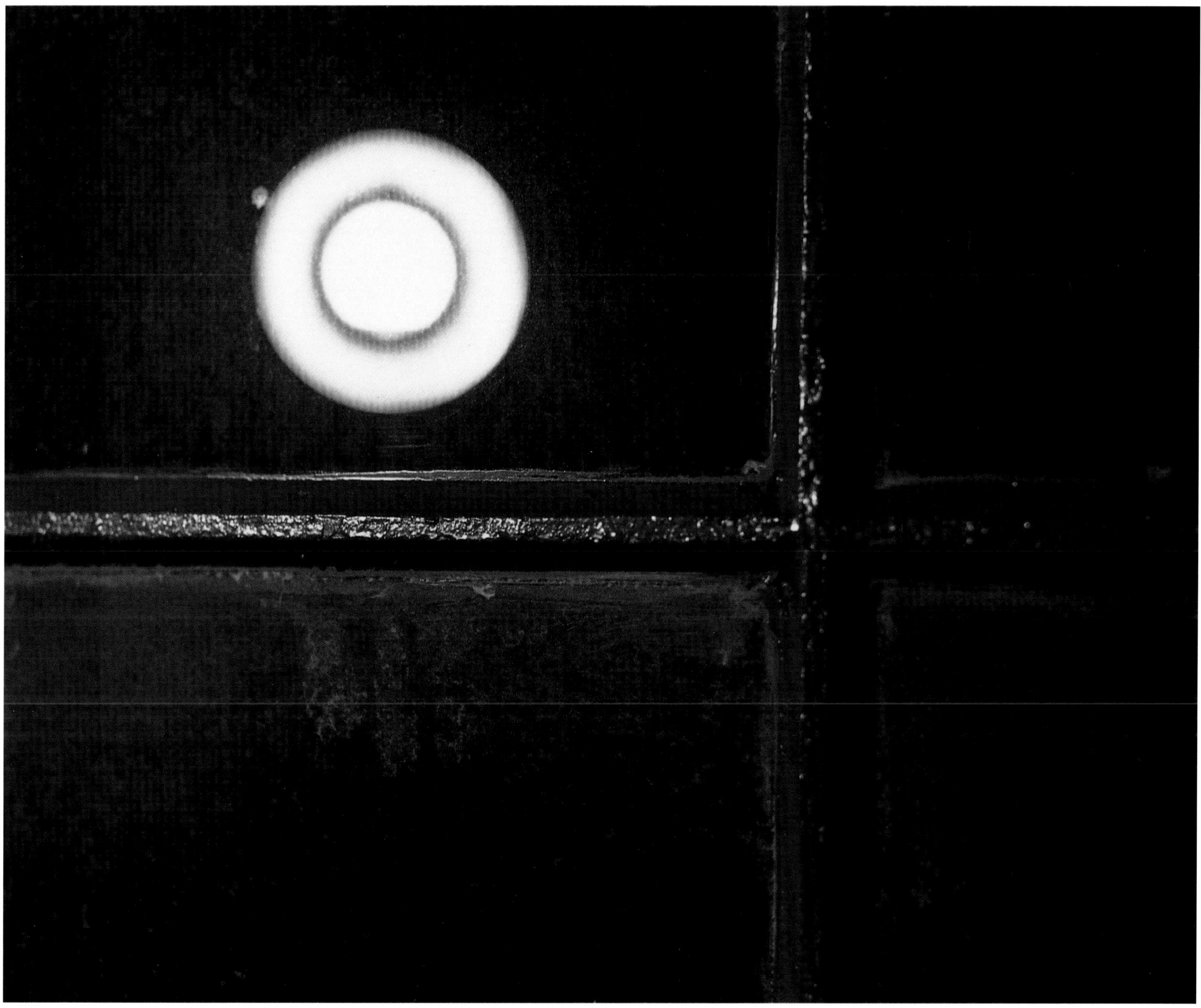

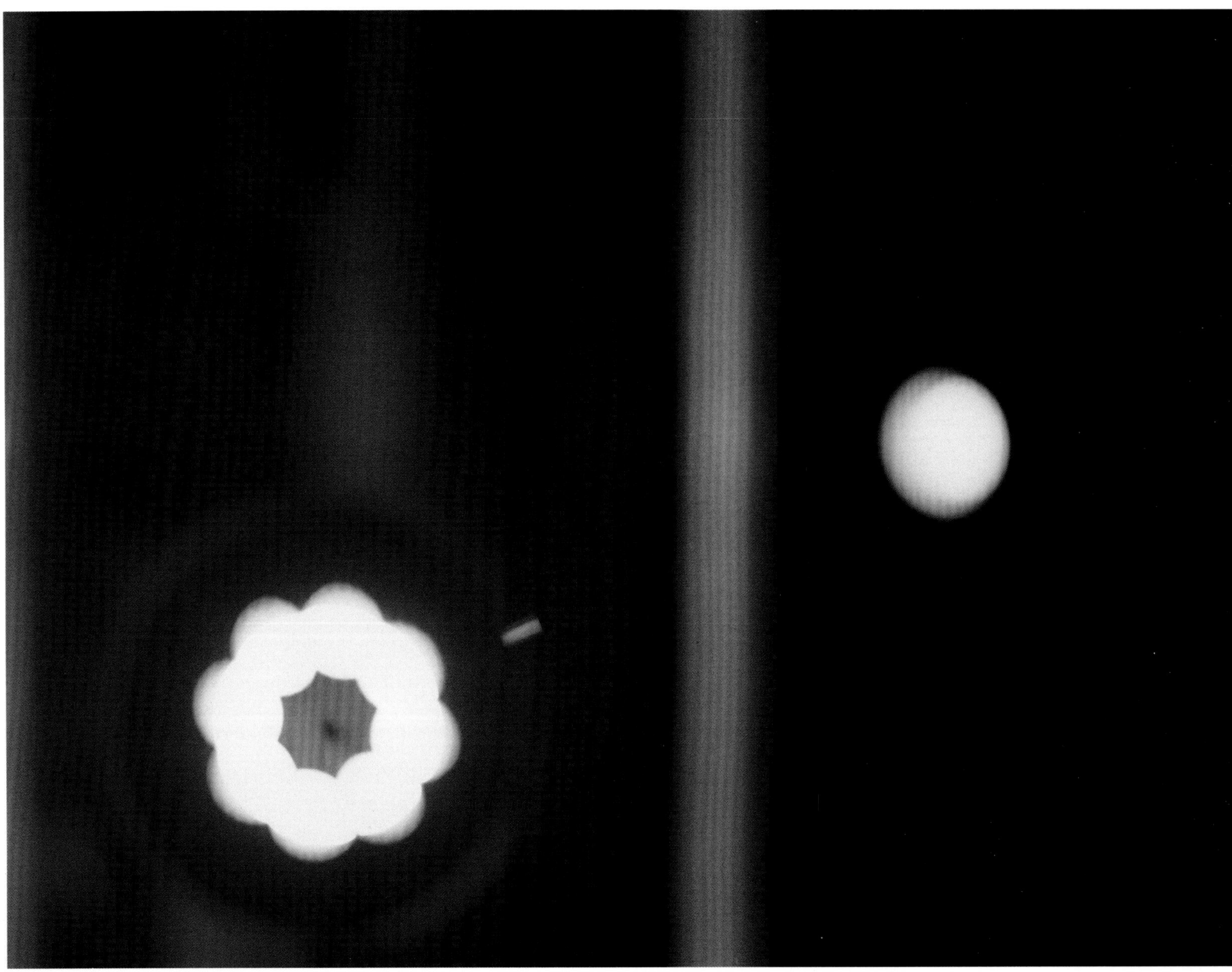

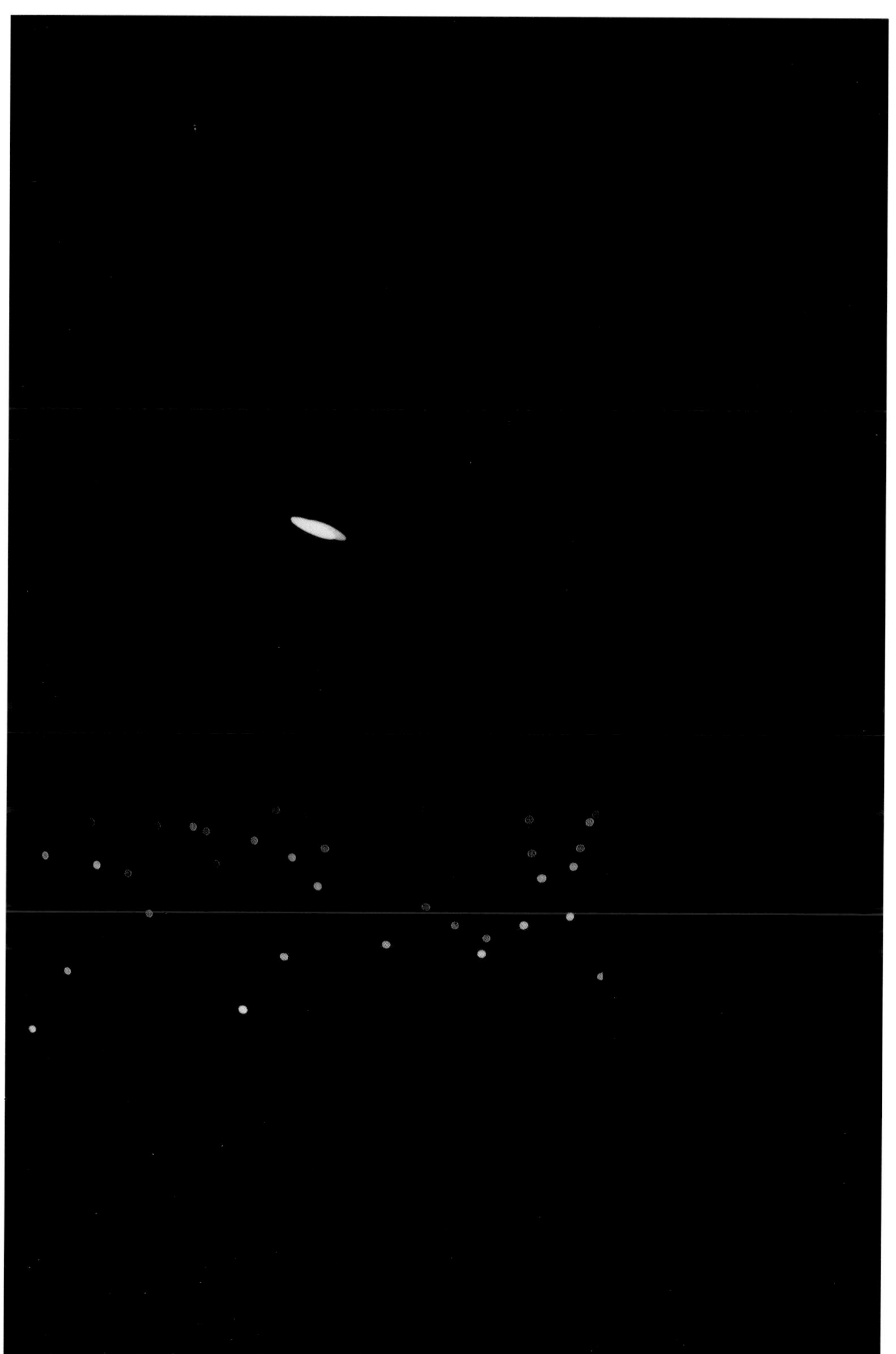

A Few Words

I move through the book turning pages; there is something homely about the route. Photographs dwelling in a book: yes, I'm at home with the route that takes me through the book, from beginning to end. And yes, I'm at home with the thought of photographs dwelling in books.

But, suddenly, my homely thoughts are interrupted. As I move from one photograph to another my thinking ceases to go around things in the same way. I receive, from the photographs, a sudden jolt. A familiar circuit breaks and new circuits, unthought of circuits, open up. The feeling is that my thought has been put into motion. And this feeling brings with it a brain wave: it's not that I'm thinking a thought which has somehow existed before its thinking, a thought which has, as it were, already been 'said', it's more that I'm feeling the sensation of the movement of thought. The very process itself. It's as if there is the Saying without the Said.

A brain wave; the opening up of new cerebal circuits; thought navigating uncharted channels; thought twisting, perhaps fissuring, perhaps folding, the matter of the brain; connections; short-circuits; new pathways; new synapses. But wait, as I describe the affect the photographs produce, a philosopher gently taps me on the shoulder: your description is producing an image of thought.

– No, I can't leave the philosopher out of the picture.

This is all the philosopher is saying: there is an image of thought that, as it unfolds, branches out, mutates and refolds, inspires a need to keep on creating. The philosopher looks to the brain for the image. The brain, that is, as an uncertain system. It isn't just an intellectual matter, the brain's emotive, impassioned too.

And then there is another brain wave: for all their homely references aren't Lynn Silverman's photographs, like Gilles Deleuze's brain, an uncertain system? Doesn't the journey through the photographs continually and unpredictably create new circuits, new folds, as it were, in the brain? No, we can never quite predict the outcome in advance.

This is what the philosopher is saying: creating new circuits in art means creating them in the brain too.

But wait, is the philosopher suggesting to me that the image of thought we hold affects the way we think (and feel)?

You have moved through this book and then, at the end, you discover a few words. What are these words going to do? Are they going to explain? Are they going to comment? Are they going to provide a bit of a discussion upon the photographs that have just been seen?

For some people, thinking is just a bit of a discussion.

– 'OK, it's a stupid image, but even stupid people have an image of thought.' [1]

Are the stupid ignorant? Do they need enlightenment? Indeed, are the ignorant those who remain 'in the dark'? But wait, the questions lead me to another image of thought. This time, the image of thought as a shedding of light. Thought is that which sheds a light upon things. But come, what does this image presume? It presumes that darkness is ignorance. For their nocturnal laziness the ignorant are condemned. To shed a light is to illuminate darkness. Oh victory of light over ignorant shadow! And so the movement goes, from dark to light.

But wait, do we find this sort of movement as we move through the photographic images which compose this book?

I don't think so.

To cause darkness to be illuminated; to shed a light: for this image of thought light remains outside of, exterior to, darkness. It has to be an exterior light, if not there is the danger of being affected by darkness, infected with ignorance. Only an exterior light can cause darkness to be illuminated. But wait, is it this image of thought which makes us think that causes remain exterior to, transcendent of, effects? And, moreover, what does this image of (external) cause do?

– It renders the world hierarchical. The productions of the world are beholden to a power which is above and beyond the world.

But do the photographs reproduced in this book reproduce the superior cause of an exterior light?

– No, the photographs don't make me think that way.

I would be a fool to deny that the photographs were caused by light. OK, it's what we call an artificial light but isn't the real question this: has the light caused the illumination of darkness?

Again I say, I don't think so. The photographs don't make me think in that way; they don't make me feel that my thought is beholden to a superior exterior cause.

I look at the photographs and then, again, the feeling of a brain wave: the photographs haven't been caused by an exterior light, there is no image of light illuminating darkness, there is no image of a light lighting up the whole scene, and this suggests to me that these photographic images have been caused by an *interior* light. The photographs make me think of a cause which remains internal to its productions. Or, I could put it this way: the light-cause has been folded into the photographic production. Yes, think of how a light-cause has been folded into the production of dark black coal. Yes, think of how causes and forces remain non-separable from their effects or manifestations.

A non-transcendent light and a cause which ceases to remain beyond and above its effects or expressions: the very thought makes me think that the Said can never remain external to its Saying.

The lights within the photographic images haven't sought to illuminate darkness; there has been no pretence to be beyond, outside of, darkness. Yes, with these photographic images I have the feeling of a coexistence. Of both light and dark. Rather than one gaining dominion over the other, both remaining interior to each other.

We may think that life is unthinkable without light; we may indeed bathe beauty in the presence of light; yet isn't life, and indeed beauty, always moving through a spectrum of light and dark? The photographs in this book don't make me afraid of the dark and neither do they make me afraid to speak of the beauty of a darkness which fills half the photographic image.

And here I can't exclude the philosopher who says that there is as much shadow in clarity as there is light in what we call shadow. It is, quite simply, a brain wave to realise that 'things that are clear take as long to see as things thought to be shady, which are sometimes as clear as the clear things.'[2]

Do I have this brain wave as I look at the dark and light which coexist in the photographs which compose this book?

– Yes, the photographs make me think so; they make me feel so.

1. See Gilles Deleuze, *Negotiations*, Columbia University Press, New York, 1995, pp 60-61 and pp l48-149.

2. Michel Serres, *Rome: The Book of Foundations*, Stanford University Press, California, 1991, p73.

Postscript

I have been invited to say my thoughts. The photographs certainly invite us to say our thoughts yet I feel that the thoughts they ask us to say are ones that don't remain transcendent of the process of thinking itself. Upon saying this, could it be said that with these few words my thoughts have found a home?

In no way would I want to think that the photographs dwelling in this book are reducible to a few words. It may be thought that words are the dwelling place of thought but then, with a sudden jolt, you encounter a word that, like the photographs here in this book, interrupts your homely thoughts. The route that carries you into the dwelling suddenly, stochastically, swerves, bifurcates. And then you find yourself en route to the thought that words and thoughts and the photographs in this book and the being of the book itself and being itself are irreducible to the poetics of dwelling. And who knows who will laugh at you. And who knows where the route will take you. Perhaps to the very last image in this book. Perhaps to an interior where darkness and night and shadow have ceased to be conceived as that which has missing from it, is homeless with regard to, the house and home of light. I wonder.

I wonder if I have made myself clear.

Yve Lomax

acknowledgements

The realisation of this project in book form was made possible
with the encouragement and creative input of Dewi Lewis.
Cheryl Reynold's enthusiasm and long-standing commitment were
central to the production of an exhibition of these photographs.
I am also grateful to Gloria Chalmers for her support.

Thanks to Oded and Jackie Shimshon, Jill Mustchin, Joe Hallam, Sissi Loftin
and Janet Brocklehurst for contributing an assortment of lamps.
My husband, John Penny, was helpful in critical as well as practical matters.

In particular, I want to acknowledge the generosity of
Rhiannon Williams in whose home I spent hours photographing.
It is to Rhiannon that this book is dedicated.

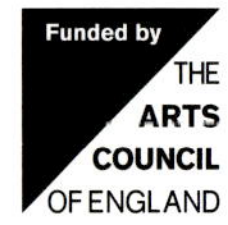

First published in the United Kingdom in 1997 by
Dewi Lewis Publishing
8 Broomfield Road
Heaton Moor
Stockport SK4 4ND
England
0161 442 9450

ISBN: 1 899235 70 1

Design & Artwork Production: Dewi Lewis Publishing
Reprographics: Leeds Photo Litho
Print: Jackson Wilson, Leeds

The exhibition Interior Light is toured by Impressions Gallery, York